Pasta Planner

A Pasta Cookbook with Delicious Pasta
Recipes for Every Day of the Week

By
BookSumo Press

Published by
http://www.booksumo.com

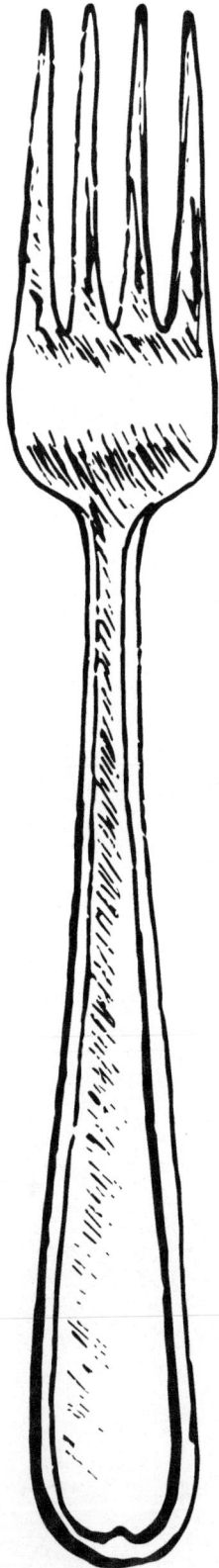

Table of Contents

Multi-Grain Mushrooms Pasta 7

Jalapeno Spaghetti 8

Poppy Pasta and Sesame Salad 10

Camillus Cheddar Pasta 11

80-Minute Spaghetti Bolognese 12

Lisette's Pizza 13

Vegan Meatballs with Spaghetti 14

5-Ingrdient Spaghetti 15

Cheesy Garlic Spaghetti 16

Pesto Spaghetti with Chicken Meatballs 17

Sage Spaghetti with Potatoes 18

Spaghetti with Broccoli Sauce 19

Sophomore Year Spaghetti 20

Arabian Spaghetti 21

Spaghetti Drums 22

Tuesday's Dinner 23

Arizona Spaghetti 24

Spaghetti Garden Party 25

Spaghetti Japanese House Style 26

Honolulu Pineapple Spaghetti 27

Spaghetti with Eggplant Sauce 28

Cancun Spaghetti 29

Italian Puttanesca Pasta 30

Maria's Alla-Mamma Pasta 31

5-Ingredient Spaghetti II 32

Pecorino Romano Spaghetti 33

Amish Friendship Omelets 34

Pennsylvania Sunset Herbed Glazed Spaghetti 35

Backroad Oven Beef and Spaghetti Casserole 36

Herbed Spaghetti 37

Mexican Spaghetti with Corn Casserole 38

Healthier Turkey Lasagna 39

No-Noodle Lasagna 40

No-Bake 3 Cheese Lasagna 41

Garden Lasagna III 42

Pretty Easy Lasagna 43

Microwave Mexican Lasagna 44

Italian Seashells Salad 45

Hermosa Ranch Pasta Salad 46

Mexican Style Rotini Salad 47

French Taco Spirals Salad 48

Italian Spring Pasta Salad 49

Fruity Salmon Macaroni Salad with Yogurt Dressing 50

Balsamic Romaine Shells Salad 51

Fruity Curry Shells Salad 52

Garbanzo Bows Pasta 53

Broccoli Romano Ravioli Salad 54

Cocktail Shrimp Macaroni Salad 55

Tri-colored Greek Style Pasta Salad 56

Hot Pasta Spirals Salad 57

Rotini Crabmeat Salad 58

Greek Rotini Salad with Lemon Dressing 59

French Inspired Noodles 60

Wednesday's Dinner 61

Eggy-Weggy Noodle Bake 62

Chicken and Onion Egg Noodle Dump Dinner 63

Noodles Soup Tunisian Style 64

Mock Hamburger Helper 65

Polish Noodles 66

Chinese Noodle Salad 67

Country Egg Noodle Casserole 68

Butter Parmesan Noodles 69

Creamy Noodles Milanese 70

Little Tike Noodles 71

Tomato Soup and Noodles 72

Japanese Style Egg Noodle 73

Gnocchi Comfort Food 74

Fiesta Gnocchi 75

Restaurant Style Gnocchi 77

Lory Beth's Favorite 78

Southern Italian Country Gnocchi 79

Rustic Cottage Gnocchi 80

Sweet Rice Gnocchi 81

Saint Anne's Feast Gnocchi 82

5-Ingredient Gnocchi 83

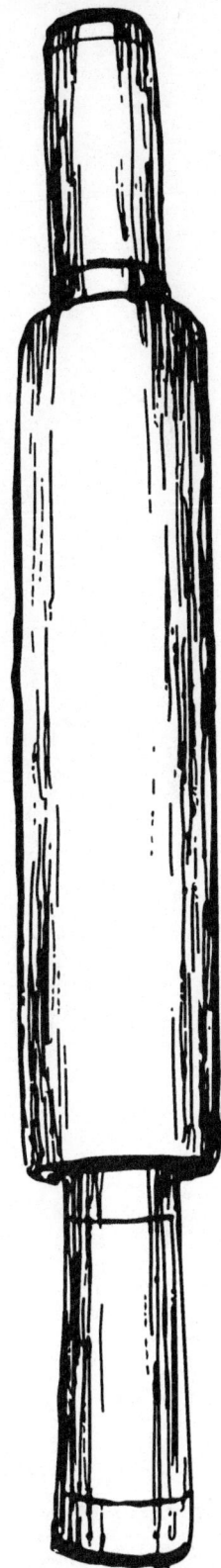

Whipped Cream Gnocchi 84

Tuesday's Lunch 85

Gnocchi Soup 101 86

How to Make Gnocchi 87

Gnocchi British Style 88

Hot Potato Gnocchi 89

Multi-Grain
Mushrooms Pasta

Prep Time: 15 mins
Total Time: 30 mins

Servings per Recipe: 6
Calories	130.5
Fat	8.7g
Cholesterol	15.6mg
Sodium	275.7mg
Carbohydrates	5.6g
Protein	8.4g

Ingredients

12 oz. multi-grain spaghetti
2 tbsp olive oil
8 garlic cloves, minced
2 tbsp basil
1 tbsp oregano
8 oz. sliced mushrooms
1 yellow pepper, sliced into matchsticks

1 pint grape tomatoes, sliced in halves
1 (14 oz.) cans Italian tomatoes
5 oz. parmesan cheese, grated

Directions

1. Prepare the spaghetti by following the instructions on the package. Drain it.
2. Place a pan over medium heat. Heat in it the oil. Cook in it the garlic, basil, and oregano for 12 min.
3. Stir in the mushrooms, pepper, and tomatoes. Cook them for 6 to 8 min.
4. Add the spaghetti and toss it to coat. Add the parmesan cheese and stir it until it melts.
5. Serve your spaghetti warm.
6. Enjoy.

JALAPENO
Spaghetti

Prep Time: 45 mins
Total Time: 45 mins

Servings per Recipe: 8

Calories	585.1
Fat	26.0g
Cholesterol	88.7mg
Sodium	731.6mg
Carbohydrates	54.6g
Protein	31.3g

Ingredients

1 lb. spaghetti
salt
1 tbsp extra virgin olive oil
3 slices turkey bacon, chopped
1 lb. lean ground beef
1 medium onion, chopped
3 - 4 garlic cloves, chopped
fresh ground black pepper
2 tsp hot sauce
1 tbsp Worcestershire sauce
1 tbsp chili powder
1/2 tbsp ground cumin

5 oz. beef broth
14 oz. crushed fire-roasted tomatoes
8 oz. tomato sauce
2 tbsp butter
2 tbsp flour
1 C. chicken stock
1 C. milk
2 1/2 C. shredded cheddar cheese
1/4 C. pickled jalapeno pepper, chopped
4 scallions, chopped

Directions

1. Prepare the spaghetti by following the instructions on the package. Drain it.
2. To make the tomato sauce:
3. Place a large skillet over medium heat. Heat in it the oil. Cook in it the bacon for 6 min.
4. Drain it and place it aside.
5. Stir in the sirloin and cook it for 5 min. Stir in the garlic with onion, hot sauce, Worcestershire, chili powder and cumin, a pinch of salt and pepper.
6. Let them cook for 6 min. Stir in the broth and let them cook for 1 to 2 min.
7. Stir in the tomato with tomato sauce. Cook them until they start boiling for 6 min. Stir in the spaghetti.
8. To make the cheese sauce:
9. Heat in it the butter until it melts. Mix in the flour and cook it for 60 seconds.
10. Add the chicken stock while whisking them all the time followed by the milk. Let them

cook for 2 to 3 min.

11. Add the cheese and stir it until it melts. Fold the scallions with jalapenos, a pinch of salt and pepper.

12. Divide the spaghetti between serving plates. Drizzle the cheese sauce on top then serve them right away.

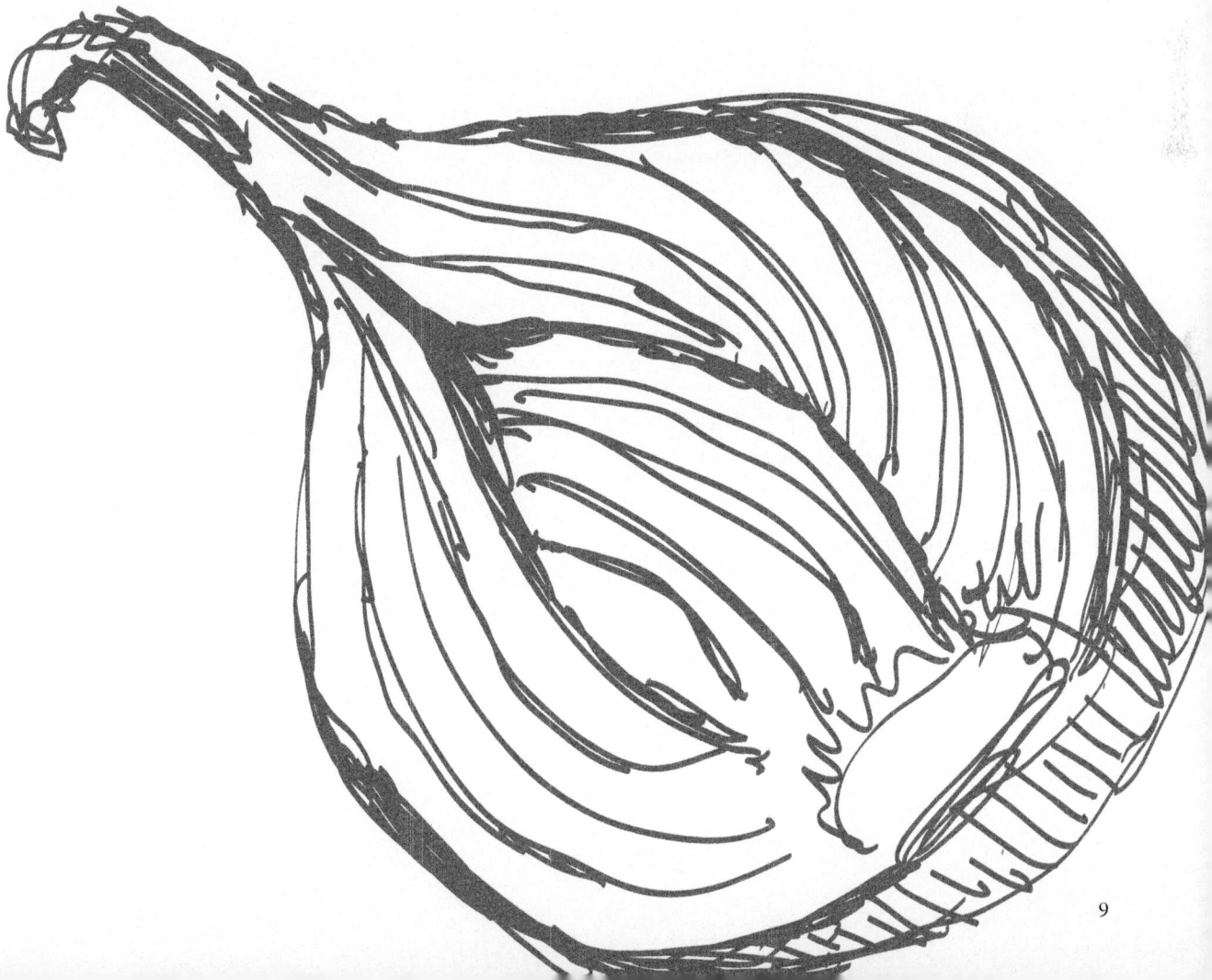

13. Enjoy.

POPPY
Pasta and Sesame Salad

Prep Time: 10 mins
Total Time: 22 mins

Servings per Recipe: 4

Calories	683.1
Fat	22.8g
Cholesterol	0.0mg
Sodium	737.0mg
Carbohydrates	103.3g
Protein	17.3g

Ingredients

1 (16 oz.) packages spaghetti, broken in half
3 medium tomatoes, diced
1 cucumber, seeded and diced
1 green pepper, diced
1 red onion, diced
1 (10 oz.) bottles Italian salad dressing

1 tsp poppy seed
1/2 tsp paprika
1/4 tsp celery salt
1 tsp sesame seeds
1/8 tsp garlic salt

Directions

1. Prepare the spaghetti by following the instructions on the package. Drain it.
2. Get a mixing bowl: Toss in it the veggies with spaghetti.
3. Get a mixing bowl: Whisk in it the Italian dressing with poppy seed, paprika, celery salt, sesame seeds and garlic salt.
4. Add the dressing to the pasta then toss it to coat. Chill the salad in the fridge for few hours then serve it.
5. Enjoy.

Camillus
Cheddar Pasta

🥣 Prep Time: 10 mins
🕐 Total Time: 30 mins

Servings per Recipe: 6
Calories	319.6
Fat	13.1g
Cholesterol	39.7mg
Sodium	485.6mg
Carbohydrates	35.3g
Protein	15.3g

Ingredients

1/2 lb. spaghetti
1/2 lb. sharp to old cheddar cheese, cubed
1 large onion, chopped
1 (19 oz.) cans tomato juice

butter
salt and pepper

Directions

1. Before you do anything, preheat the oven to 350 F.
2. Prepare the spaghetti by following the instructions on the package. Drain it.
3. Place a saucepan over medium heat. Heat in it the oil. Sauté in it the onion with a pinch of salt for 3 min.
4. Stir in the tomato juice. Cook them until they start boiling. Stir in the cheese until it melts.
5. Add the spaghetti and toss them to coat.
6. Pour the spaghetti mixture in a baking dish. Place it in the oven and let it cook for 12 min 16 min.
7. Enjoy.

80-MINUTE
Spaghetti Bolognese

Prep Time: 50 mins
Total Time: 1 hr 20 mins

Servings per Recipe: 8
Calories	589.8
Fat	22.5g
Cholesterol	82.7mg
Sodium	1053.9mg
Carbohydrates	62.6g
Protein	34.5g

Ingredients

1 lb. spaghetti, cooked
2 lbs. ground beef, cooked and drained
3 garlic cloves, diced
2 large onions, diced
1 green pepper, diced
2 celery ribs, diced
1 lb. mushroom, sliced
1/2 tsp chili flakes
1 1/2 tsp dried basil

1 1/2 tsp dried oregano
1 tsp salt
1 tsp pepper
2 bay leaves
1 (28 oz.) cans diced tomatoes
1 (6 oz.) cans tomato paste
2 (10 oz.) cans cream of chicken soup

Directions

1. Prepare the spaghetti by following the instructions on the package. Drain it.
2. Place a pan over medium heat. Cook in it the beef for 8 min. Stir in the garlic, onion, green pepper, celery, mushrooms, and spices.
3. Cook them for 22 min over low heat. Stir in the tomatoes with tomato paste, chicken soup, a pinch of salt and pepper.
4. Let them cook until they start boiling. Lower the heat and let them cook for 22 min.
5. Serve your chili spaghetti warm with some extra spaghetti sauce
6. Enjoy.

Lisette's
Pizza

🥣 Prep Time: 15 mins
🕐 Total Time: 1 hr 5 mins

Servings per Recipe: 8
Calories	451.9
Fat	18.3g
Cholesterol	107.6mg
Sodium	1163.6mg
Carbohydrates	41.1g
Protein	30.6g

Ingredients

8 oz. spaghetti, broken in half
2 eggs
1/2 C. skim milk
3 C. shredded part-skim mozzarella
cheese
8 oz. fresh spinach, cooked and chopped
1/2 tsp garlic powder

1 (32 oz.) jars spaghetti sauce, uncooked
Garnish
2 C. cooked broccoli florets
1 medium zucchini, sliced

Directions

1. Before you do anything, preheat the oven to 425 F.
2. Prepare the spaghetti by following the instructions on the package. Drain it.
3. Get a mixing bowl: Whisk in it the eggs. Mix in it the milk with 1 C. of mozzarella cheese, garlic powder and spinach.
4. Add the uncooked spaghetti and combine them well. Pour the mixture into a greased baking dish.
5. Place the casserole in the oven and let it cook for 16 min. Pour over it the spaghetti sauce.
6. Lay the broccoli and zucchini on top followed by the mozzarella cheese.
7. Lower the oven heat to 350 F. Place the casserole in the oven and let it cook for 36 min.
8. Allow the spaghetti casserole to sit for 6 min. Serve it warm.
9. Enjoy.

VEGAN
Meatballs with Spaghetti

Prep Time: 15 mins
Total Time: 45 mins

Servings per Recipe: 1
Calories	82.0
Fat	5.3g
Cholesterol	10.3mg
Sodium	131.1mg
Carbohydrates	4.5g
Protein	4.9g

Ingredients

3 tbsp olive oil
1 large onion, chopped
3 garlic cloves, minced
1 large carrot, grated
1 green pepper, chopped
1 1/2 tsp dried basil
3/4 tsp dried oregano
2 large eggs
1 C. whole wheat breadcrumbs

3/4 C. walnuts, ground
1/4 C. fresh parsley, chopped
1 1/2 tbsp Dijon mustard
1 1/2 tbsp sesame oil
3 tbsp soy sauce
salt and black pepper,
3 lbs. firm tofu, pressed and crumbled

Directions

1. Before you do anything, preheat the oven to 350 F.
2. Place a pan over medium heat. Heat in it the oil. Cook in it the onion, carrot, pepper, garlic and dried herbs for 11 min.
3. Get a mixing bowl: Whisk in it the eggs with bread crumbs, walnuts, parsley, mustard, sesame oil, and soy sauce.
4. Mix in the tofu with cooked veggies. Shape the mixture into 1 1/2 inch meatballs. Place them on a lined up baking tray.
5. Place it in the oven and let it cook for 22 to 28 min.
6. Serve your meatballs warm with some spaghetti sauce and cooked spaghetti.
7. Enjoy.

5-Ingrdient
Spaghetti

🍳 Prep Time: 20 mins
🕐 Total Time: 35 mins

Servings per Recipe: 4
Calories   512.6
Fat   21.9g
Cholesterol   94.9mg
Sodium   857.8mg
Carbohydrates   45.3g
Protein   31.2g

Ingredients

1 lb. lean ground beef
0.5 (4 oz.) packages Cream Cheese, cubed
0.5 (8 oz.) packages spaghetti, cooked and drained

1 (24 oz.) jars Italian sauce
2 tbsp grated parmesan cheese

Directions

1. Place a pan over medium heat. Brown in it the beef for 8 min. Discard the fat.
2. Add the Italian sauce with cream cheese, a pinch of salt and pepper. Lower the heat and let them cook for 4 min.
3. Stir in the spaghetti with parmesan cheese. Cook them for 1 to 2 min until the cheese melts.
4. Serve your cream spaghetti warm with some chopped herbs.
5. Enjoy.

CHEESY
Garlic Spaghetti

Prep Time: 10 mins
Total Time: 25 mins

Servings per Recipe: 1

Calories	1713.5
Fat	92.9 g
Cholesterol	186.7 mg
Sodium	1283.8 mg
Carbohydrates	175.2 g
Protein	43.9 g

Ingredients

8 oz. spaghetti
4 tbsp butter
2 tbsp olive oil
2 garlic cloves, minced

2 oz. feta cheese
1/8 C. parmesan cheese

Directions

1. Prepare the spaghetti by following the instructions on the package. Drain it.
2. Place a pan over medium heat. Heat in it the butter with oil. Cook in it the garlic for 1 min.
3. Stir in the spaghetti. Sprinkle the parmesan and feta cheese on top. Toss them to coat.
4. Serve your cheesy spaghetti warm.
5. Enjoy.

Pesto
Spaghetti with Chicken Meatballs

🥣 Prep Time: 15 mins

🕐 Total Time: 30 mins

Servings per Recipe: 4

Calories	779.5
Fat	30.3g
Cholesterol	182.5mg
Sodium	338.0mg
Carbohydrates	85.6g
Protein	39.4g

Ingredients

Noodles
3/4 lb. spaghetti
2 tbsp olive oil
1 C. chicken stock
1/2 C. cream
1/4 C. Parmigiano-Reggiano cheese, grated
1/4 C. fresh basil, chopped
salt and pepper

Meat
1 lb. ground chicken
1/3 C. store-bought pesto sauce
1/3 C. breadcrumbs
1 egg
1/2 C. flour

Directions

1. Prepare the spaghetti by following the instructions on the package. Drain it.
2. To make the meatballs:
3. Get a mixing bowl: Mix in it the chicken with pesto sauce, breadcrumbs, egg, a pinch of salt and pepper.
4. Shape the mixture into bite size meatballs. Toss them slightly in the flour then place them on a cookie sheet.
5. Place a saucepan over medium heat. Heat in it the oil. Cook in it the meatballs until they become golden brown. Stir in the cream with stock.
6. Cook them until they start boiling. Lower the heat and let them cook for 10 to 16 min or until the meatballs are done.
7. Stir in the basil with parmesan cheese. Stir it until it melts. Place the spaghetti on serving plates. Spoon the meatballs with their sauce on top.
8. Enjoy.

SAGE
Spaghetti with Potatoes

Prep Time: 10 mins
Total Time: 50 mins

Servings per Recipe: 6
Calories   819.2
Fat   6.6g
Cholesterol   14.6mg
Sodium   290.4mg
Carbohydrates   161.5g
Protein   29.1g

Ingredients

8 large potatoes, peeled and sliced
olive oil
1 tsp dried thyme
1 large onion, sliced
4 garlic cloves,   chopped
1/2 C. sage leaf
17.5 spaghetti
1 1/2 C. vegetable stock
sea salt

fresh ground black pepper
1 large lemon, juice
3.5oz. parmesan cheese, shaved

Directions

1. Before you do anything, preheat the oven to 400 F.
2. Lay the potato slices on a lined up baking sheet. Toss in it the thyme with a drizzle of olive oil.
3. Place the pan in the oven and let it cook for 16 to 21 min until they become golden brown.
4. Place a saucepan over medium heat. Heat in it 1 tbsp of olive oil. Cook in it the garlic with onion for 3 min.
5. Stir in the sage and cook them for 30 sec. Add the spaghetti and stir them well.
6. Stir in the stock with a pinch of salt and pepper. Let them cook for 2 to 3 min.
7. Remove the potato pan from the oven. Mix in it the potato slices with lemon juice. Bake them for an extra 2 min.
8. Serve your spaghetti warm with the crunchy potato and some bread rolls.
9. Enjoy.

Spaghetti
with Broccoli Sauce

🥄 Prep Time: 15 mins

🕐 Total Time: 30 mins

Servings per Recipe: 4

Calories	855.3
Fat	38.6g
Cholesterol	110.4mg
Sodium	1646.6mg
Carbohydrates	98.5g
Protein	29.8g

Ingredients

1 lb. spaghetti, cooked
24 oz. half-and-half cream
1/4 C. butter
1/2 lb. small broccoli floret
1 C. sliced mushrooms
1/4 C. minced parsley
1 1/2 tsp fresh minced garlic

1 tbsp black pepper
2 tsp salt
3/4 C. grated parmesan cheese

Directions

1. Place a small saucepan over medium heat. cream, butter, broccoli, mushrooms, parsley and seasonings.
2. Cook them for 4 to 6 min. Let them cook until they start boiling. Stir in the spaghetti.
3. Lower the heat and let them cook for 2 to 3 min.
4. Adjust the seasoning of your spaghetti then serve it warm.
5. Enjoy.

SOPHOMORE YEAR
Spaghetti

Prep Time: 15 mins
Total Time: 45 mins

Servings per Recipe: 8
Calories	542.2
Fat	22.8g
Cholesterol	81.6mg
Sodium	1384.8mg
Carbohydrates	56.0g
Protein	27.3g

Ingredients

1 green pepper, diced
1 C. celery, diced
1 medium onion, diced
2 tbsp butter
2 C. cooked chicken, boned
1/4 C. pimiento
1/4-1/2 C. mushroom, sliced canned
1 lb. spaghetti

1 (10 1/2 oz.) cans cream of mushroom soup
1 (10 1/2 oz.) cans cream of chicken soup
1 lb. Velveeta cheese
grated cheddar cheese

Directions

1. Before you do anything, preheat the oven to 350 F.
2. Heat the broth in a large saucepan until it starts boiling. Cook in it the spaghetti for 7 to 8 min until it becomes dente.
3. Before you do anything, preheat the oven to 350 F.
4. Place a pan over medium heat. Heat in it the oil. Cook in it the pepper, celery, and onion in butter for 3 min.
5. Place a small saucepan over medium heat. Combine in it the soups with cheese.
6. Let them cook until the cheese melts. Stir in the spaghetti with cooked veggies, a pinch of salt and pepper.
7. Pour the mixture into a casserole dish. Place it in the oven and let it cook for 32 to 36 min.
8. Serve your spaghetti casserole warm and enjoy.
9. Enjoy.

Arabian
Spaghetti

🥣 Prep Time: 40 mins
🕐 Total Time: 2 hrs 10 mins

Servings per Recipe: 8
Calories	698.4
Fat	38.2g
Cholesterol	121.9mg
Sodium	119.5mg
Carbohydrates	49.5g
Protein	38.2g

Ingredients

1 whole chicken, 3 lb.
2 tbsp extra-virgin olive oil
1 tsp cumin
1/2 tsp allspice
1/4 tsp cayenne pepper
salt & ground black pepper
chicken broth

1/3 C. raisins, soaked in warm water and drained
1/2 C. pine nuts, lightly toasted
1 lb. spaghetti
1/4 C. slivered almonds, toasted
1/4 C. fresh parsley leaves, chopped

Directions

1. Before you do anything, preheat the oven to 350 F. Grease a baking sheet and place it aside. Get a small mixing bowl: Mix in it the oil with cumin, allspice and pepper. Coat the whole chicken with the spice mix.
2. Season it with some salt and pepper. Place it in roasting dish with the breast facing down. Cook it in the oven for 1 h.
3. Flip the chicken and let it cook for an extra 35 min. Allow it to cool down for a while. Shred the chicken and reserve the meat.
4. Place a large saucepan over medium heat. Pour in it all the chicken juice from the pan and add more water to make 1 C. of it.
5. Stir in the raisins and the pine nuts, a pinch of salt and pepper. Cook them until they start simmering.
6. Lower the heat and let them cook until the sauce reduces and becomes slightly thick. Prepare the pasta by following the instructions on the package. Drain it. Add the pasta with shredded chicken to the raisins sauce. Toss them to coat.
7. Serve your pasta warm. Garnish it with parsley and almonds.
8. Enjoy.

SPAGHETTI
Drums

Prep Time: 5 mins
Total Time: 2 hrs 5 mins

Servings per Recipe: 4
Calories   665.0
Fat   36.0g
Cholesterol   242.5mg
Sodium   989.1mg
Carbohydrates   25.6g
Protein   56.2g

Ingredients

7 chicken legs
1 (28 oz.) cans crushed tomatoes
1 (8 oz.) cans tomato sauce
1/4 C. broth
1 large onion, diced
2 garlic cloves, minced
1 tsp basil
1/2 tsp oregano

salt and pepper
celery salt
3 carrots, peeled and diced
olive oil

Directions

1. Season the chicken legs with some salt and pepper.
2. Place a large pot over medium heat. Heat in it the oil. Cook in it the chicken legs until they become golden brown.
3. Drain the chicken legs and discard their skin. Stir them back into the pot with garlic, and onion. Cook them for 3 to 4 min.
4. Stir in the broth and cook them for 2 to 3 min. Stir in the carrots and cook them until the broth becomes thick.
5. Stir in the tomato with spices and tomato sauce. Lower the heat and let them cook for 120 min.
6. Once the time is up, serve your chicken legs stew with some spaghetti.
7. Enjoy.

Tuesday's
Dinner (Lemon Pasta with Chicken Cutlets)

🥣 Prep Time: 1 hr 15 mins
🕐 Total Time: 1 hr 45 mins

Servings per Recipe: 5
Calories	435.2
Fat	20.4g
Cholesterol	58.1mg
Sodium	526.8mg
Carbohydrates	34.4g
Protein	28.4g

Ingredients

1 lb. chicken breast, cut into pieces
3 lemons, juice
4 tbsp oil
1 tsp minced onion, dried
1 tsp minced garlic
1/2 tsp black pepper
1/2 tsp oregano

1 tsp salt
8 oz. thin spaghetti

Directions

1. Get a mixing bowl: Whisk in it the lemon juice with salt, oregano, garlic, onion, and oil.
2. Get a zip lock bag: Place in it the chicken and with the lemon mixture. Seal the bag and shake it to coat.
3. Let it sit for 60 min in the fridge.
4. Before you do anything, preheat the oven to 350 F.
5. Pour the chicken with the marinade into a greased baking dish. Place it in the oven and let it cook for 32 min.
6. Prepare the spaghetti by following the instructions on the package. Drain it.
7. Spoon the baked lemon chicken over the spaghetti then serve it warm
8. Enjoy.

ARIZONA
Spaghetti

Prep Time: 15 mins
Total Time: 45 mins

Servings per Recipe: 6

Calories	238.6
Fat	5.5g
Cholesterol	12.0mg
Sodium	669.8mg
Carbohydrates	37.9g
Protein	10.1g

Ingredients

1 1/4 lbs. turkey kielbasa, ground
1 C. onion, chopped
2 tsp garlic, minced
2 tsp chili powder
1 tsp ground cumin
1 (14 1/2 oz.) cans Rotel Tomatoes, chili seasoned
3/4 C. picante sauce

1 tsp dried oregano
1 C. cheese, shredded
8 oz. spaghetti, cooked and drained

Directions

1. Place a pan over medium heat. Cook in it the crumbled sausages.
2. Stir in the onion, garlic, chili powder, and cumin for 9 min.
3. Stir in the tomatoes, picante sauce, oregano, a pinch of salt and pepper. Cook them until they start boiling.
4. Lower the heat and let the sauce cook for 18 to 22 min.
5. Place the spaghetti in serving bowl. Spoon the hot sauce over it.
6. Garnish it with shredded cheese then serve it right away.
7. Enjoy.

Spaghetti Garden Party

🍲 Prep Time: 20 mins
🕐 Total Time: 35 mins

Servings per Recipe: 5
Calories   535.7
Fat   17.2g
Cholesterol   2.6mg
Sodium   348.2mg
Carbohydrates   80.6g
Protein   15.6g

Ingredients

1 lb. spaghetti
2 tomatoes, diced
1 green pepper, seeded and diced
1 red pepper, seeded and diced
2 zucchini, diced
3 celery ribs, sliced
2 carrots, sliced
6 oz. sliced black olives, drained
1/4 C. olive oil

3 tbsp parmesan cheese
2 tsp minced garlic
1 tsp basil
salt and pepper
shredded mozzarella cheese
1 1/2 C. cooked chicken, chopped

Directions

1. Prepare the spaghetti by following the instructions on the package. Drain it.
2. Place a large pan over medium heat. Heat in it the oil. Cook in it the veggies for 6 to 10 min until it become soft.
3. Get a small mixing bowl: Whisk in it the oil, cheese, garlic, basil, salt and pepper to make the dressing.
4. Get a large mixing bowl: Toss in it the veggies with dressing. Spoon the mixture over the spaghetti.
5. Garnish your salad with some mozzarella cheese then serve it.
6. Enjoy.

SPAGHETTI
Japanese House Style

🍲 Prep Time: 20 mins
🕐 Total Time: 35 mins

Servings per Recipe: 3
Calories   388.8
Fat   4.7g
Cholesterol   47.8mg
Sodium   1337.6mg
Carbohydrates   73.8g
Protein   15.7g

Ingredients

1 small onion, chopped
1 sweet red pepper, sliced
4 medium mushrooms, sliced
1/2 head bok choy, sliced
1/2 C. green peas, frozen
1/2 C. bean sprouts
1 (6 oz.) cans water chestnuts, drained
& rinsed

1 tsp sesame oil
2 tbsp Worcestershire sauce
2 tbsp ketchup
2 tbsp light soy sauce
2 tbsp oyster sauce
6 oz. Japanese noodles

Directions

1. Before you do anything, preheat the oven to 450 F. Grease a baking sheet and place it aside.

2. Get a mixing bowl: Whisk in it the ketchup with soy, Worcestershire, and oyster sauces.

3. Prepare the spaghetti by following the instructions on the package. Drain it.

4. Place a pan over medium heat. Heat in it the oil. Cook in it the peppers, mushroom, garlic, onion, bean sprouts, and peas for 6 min.

5. Stir in the chestnuts, and bok choy. Cook them for 4 min. Stir in the noodles with ketchup sauce.

6. Adjust the seasoning of your stir fry then serve it.

7. Enjoy.

Honolulu
Pineapple Spaghetti

Prep Time: 20 mins
Total Time: 1 hr 5 mins

Servings per Recipe: 4
Calories	903.9
Fat	22.2g
Cholesterol	85.0mg
Sodium	3095.1mg
Carbohydrates	121.6g
Protein	56.1g

Ingredients

1 lb. hamburger
4 (10 1/2 oz.) cans beef gravy
1/3 C. soy sauce
1 medium onion
1 medium green pepper
1 lb. spaghetti

2 (8 oz.) cans mushrooms, drained
2 tbsp sugar
1 (6 oz.) cans pineapple chunks, drained

Directions

1. Before you do anything, preheat the oven to 350 F.
2. Cook the spaghetti by following the instructions on the package for 5 min only. Drain it.
3. Place a large pan over medium heat. Cook in it the meat with onion, mushroom and green pepper.
4. Cook them for 8 min while stirring them often. Stir in the sugar. Discard the fat.
5. Get a mixing bowl: Whisk in it the soy sauce with gravy. Stir into the meat sauce with spaghetti and pineapple, a pinch of salt and pepper.
6. Pour the mixture into a baking dish. Place it in the oven and let it cook for 35 to 46 min.
7. Serve your spaghetti dish warm.
8. Enjoy.

SPAGHETTI
with Eggplant Sauce

Prep Time: 15 mins
Total Time: 1 hr 30 mins

Servings per Recipe: 6
Calories	518.7
Fat	13.4g
Cholesterol	0.0mg
Sodium	298.2mg
Carbohydrates	86.0g
Protein	15.4g

Ingredients

17.5 oz. aubergines, diced
salt
olive oil
4 tbsp extra virgin olive oil
4 garlic cloves, chopped
2 small dried red chilies, crumbled
1 C. black olives, stoned and chopped
2 tbsp capers
1 kg large fresh tomatoes, skinned and chopped

2 tbsp tomato puree
2 tsp dried Italian seasoning
salt & ground black pepper
500 g spaghetti
fresh basil leaf
grated parmesan cheese

Directions

1. Cook the spaghetti by following the instructions on the package. Drain it.
2. Season the eggplant dices with some salt. Let them sit for 18 minutes.
3. Discard the excess water and dry them.
4. Place a pan over medium heat. Heat in it a splash of oil. Cook in it the eggplant dices until they become golden brown.
5. Drain them and place them aside. Stir in the garlic with chili flakes. Cook them for 45 seconds.
6. Stir in the olives, capers, tomatoes, puree and dried seasoning. Put on the lid and let them cook for 32 to 36 min over low heat.
7. Stir in the cooked eggplant dices with spaghetti and basil leaves.
8. Adjust the seasoning of your spaghetti then serve it warm with some grated parmesan cheese.
9. Get a mixing bowl:
10. Enjoy.

Cancun
Spaghetti

🥣 Prep Time: 20 mins
🕐 Total Time: 2 hrs 20 mins

Servings per Recipe: 4
Calories   763.3
Fat   20.2g
Cholesterol   77.1mg
Sodium   1666.5mg
Carbohydrates   105.2g
Protein   42.5g

Ingredients

1 lb. ground beef
1 medium onion, chopped
1 green bell pepper, chopped
2 garlic cloves, minced
1 (29 oz.) cans tomato puree
1 (15 1/2 oz.) cans kidney beans, drained
1 C. water
2 tbsp chili powder

1 tsp cumin
1 tsp oregano
2 tsp salt
1/4-1/2 tsp cayenne pepper
12 oz. spaghetti

Directions

1. Cook the spaghetti by following the instructions on the package for 5 min only. Drain it.
2. Place a pan over medium heat. Cook in it the beef with garlic and bell peppers for 10 min. Discard the fat.
3. Stir in the beans with spices and tomato purée. Put on the lid and let them cook for 120 min over low heat.
4. When the sauce becomes thick, turn off the heat.
5. Place the spaghetti on serving plates. Spoon the sauce over it with some grated cheese.
6. Enjoy.

ITALIAN
Puttanesca Pasta

Prep Time: 5 mins
Total Time: 20 mins

Servings per Recipe: 4
Calories   546.3
Fat   10.8g
Cholesterol   0.0mg
Sodium   334.3mg
Carbohydrates   95.6g
Protein   17.2g

Ingredients

4 garlic cloves, minced
salt
1 lb. spaghetti
2 tbsp olive oil
1 tsp red pepper flakes
4 tsp minced anchovies

1 (28 oz.) cans diced tomatoes, drained, juice reserved
3 tbsp capers, rinsed
1/2 C. black olives, pitted and chopped
1/4 C. minced fresh parsley leaves

Directions

1. Get a small mixing bowl: Stir in it 1 tbsp of water with garlic.
2. Place a large pot over medium heat. Heat in it 4 quarts of water. Add it the pasta with 1 tbsp of salt.
3. Let it cook for 8 to 10 min or until it is done. Drain it. Toss it with 1/4 C. of tomato juice.
4. Place a large pan over medium heat. Stir in it the garlic and water mix with oil, red pepper flakes and anchovies for 1 min.
5. Add the tomato and let them cook for 9 min over low heat to make the sauce.
6. Add the capers, olives, parsley, a pinch of salt and pepper. Cook them for 1 to 2 min
7. Place the spaghetti on serving plates. Spoon over it the tomato sauce then serve it hot.
8. Enjoy.

Maria's
Alla-Mamma Pasta

Prep Time: 15 mins
Total Time: 35 mins

Servings per Recipe: 4
Calories	438.2
Fat	10.4g
Cholesterol	116.6mg
Sodium	1048.6mg
Carbohydrates	59.0g
Protein	26.3g

Ingredients

10 oz. spaghetti
2 C. parsley, chopped
7 oz. shrimp
2 oz. anchovies,   chopped
1 tbsp tomato paste
1 C. tomatoes, canned
2 tbsp pepperoni, chopped

1 tbsp garlic, minced
2 tbsp olive oil
salt
pepper

Directions

1. Prepare the pasta by following the instructions on the package.
2. Place a pan over medium heat. Heat in it the oil. Cook in it the parsley with anchovies, garlic, pepperoni, and shrimps for 2 min.
3. Stir in the tomato paste and cook them for 40 seconds. Stir in the canned tomato and cook them for 3 min.
4. Toss the spaghetti with the shrimp sauce, a pinch of salt and pepper. Serve it hot.
5. Enjoy.

5-INGREDIENT
Spaghetti II

Prep Time: 6 mins
Total Time: 21 mins

Servings per Recipe: 4
Calories	610.3
Fat	8.9g
Cholesterol	0.0mg
Sodium	10.8mg
Carbohydrates	111.5g
Protein	19.1g

Ingredients

17.5 oz. spaghetti
2 onions
2 tbsp olive oil

salt
white pepper

Directions

1. Follow the instructions on the package to cook the spaghetti. Drain it.
2. Place a large pan over medium heat. Heat in it the oil. Cook in it the onion for 3 to 4 min.
3. Stir in the spaghetti with a pinch of salt and pepper. Serve it warm.
4. Enjoy.

Pecorino
Romano Spaghetti

🥣 Prep Time: 30 mins
🕐 Total Time: 50 mins

Servings per Recipe: 4
Calories   553.9
Fat   3.3g
Cholesterol   2.8mg
Sodium   77.0mg
Carbohydrates   108.7g
Protein   20.4g

Ingredients

1 1/4 lbs. spaghetti
3/4 C. pecorino Romano cheese, grated
1/4 C. Parmigiano-Reggiano cheese, grated

2 tbsp ground black pepper
kosher salt

Directions

1. Prepare the pasta by following the instructions on the package until it becomes dente for about 7 min.
2. Drain it. Place 1/2 C. of the cooking liquid aside.
3. Place a saucepan over medium heat. Combine in it the spaghetti with reserved water, and cheese.
4. Season them with some salt and pepper then toss them to coat. Serve it warm.
5. Enjoy.

AMISH FRIENDSHIP
Omelets

Prep Time: 5 mins
Total Time: 10 mins

Servings per Recipe: 2
Calories	933.8
Fat	52.5g
Cholesterol	372.0mg
Sodium	152.5mg
Carbohydrates	78.9g
Protein	35.4g

Ingredients

salt
1/2 lb. thin spaghetti
6 tbsp extra virgin olive oil
2 large garlic cloves, lightly smashed
and peeled

4 eggs
fresh ground black pepper
 grated parmesan cheese

Directions

1. Prepare the pasta by following the instructions on the package. Drain it.
2. Place a saucepan over medium heat. Heat in it 4 tbsp of oil. Sauté in it the garlic for 1 min.
3. Drain the garlic and place it aside. Stir the rest of the oil into the pan. Cook in it the eggs to your liking.
4. Use a fork to break the fried egg into pieces with garlic.
5. Add the spaghetti with a pinch of salt and pepper. Toss them to coat.
6. Serve your spaghetti hot right away.
7. Enjoy.

Pennsylvania
Sunset Herbed Glazed Spaghetti

Prep Time: 10 mins
Total Time: 40 mins

Servings per Recipe: 6
Calories	412.1
Fat	4.9g
Cholesterol	115.2mg
Sodium	120.8mg
Carbohydrates	64.1g
Protein	26.5g

Ingredients

1 lb. large shrimp, clean and divined
10 garlic cloves, peeled and minced
3 tsp olive oil
2 C. vegetable broth
2 tomatoes, sliced
1 onion, chopped
1 capsicum, chopped

2 tsp dried basil
2 tsp dried tarragon
2 tsp dried oregano
1 dash pepper
1 dash chili
1 lb. pasta, cooked

Directions

1. Place a pan over medium heat. Heat in it the oil. Cook in it the garlic for 4 min.
2. Stir in the broth and let them cook for 16 min. Stir in the tomatoes, onion, capsicum and herbs.
3. Let them cook for 7 min. Stir in the shrimp and let them cook for 3 to 5 min until it becomes pink.
4. Stir the pasta into the sauce then season it with some salt and pepper.
5. Serve your spaghetti hot with some grated cheese.
6. Enjoy.

BACKROAD
Oven Beef and Spaghetti Casserole

Prep Time: 30 mins
Total Time: 1 hr 10 mins

Servings per Recipe: 6
Calories	496.5
Fat	19.4g
Cholesterol	71.1mg
Sodium	694.3mg
Carbohydrates	54.6g
Protein	28.3g

Ingredients

1/2 lb. spaghetti, broken into pieces
1 lb. ground beef
1 medium onion, chopped
2 - 3 minced garlic cloves
1 small green bell pepper, chopped
1/2 lb. fresh mushrooms, sliced
seasoning salt
pepper
3 tbsp grated parmesan cheese

1 - 2 tsp chili powder
1 tbsp Worcestershire sauce
1 (14 oz.) cans tomatoes
1 (14 oz.) cans canned corn niblets
1 C. grated cheddar cheese
1 (10 1/2 oz.) cans tomato soup

Directions

1. Prepare the pasta by following the instructions on the package. Drain it.
2. Place a large pan over medium heat. Cook in it the ground beef with onion, garlic, green pepper and mushrooms for 8 to 10 min.
3. Discard the fat. Stir in the cheese with chili powder, tomato, corn, tomato soup and Worcestershire sauce.
4. Let them cook for 42 to 46 min. Spoon the sauce over the cooked spaghetti.
5. Garnish it with some extra cheese then serve it hot.
6. Enjoy.

Herbed
Spaghetti

Prep Time: 15 mins
Total Time: 45 mins

Servings per Recipe: 4
Calories	288.6
Fat	5.0g
Cholesterol	0.0mg
Sodium	6.9mg
Carbohydrates	51.6g
Protein	9.6g

Ingredients

2 - 4 garlic cloves, peeled and minced
3 tsp olive oil
2 C. vegetable broth
2 tomatoes, chopped
1 onion, chopped
1 red capsicums
2 tsp dried basil

2 tsp dried tarragon
2 tsp dried oregano
black pepper,
ground red chili pepper,
4 C. cooked spaghetti

Directions

1. Place a pan over medium heat. Heat in it the oil. Cook in it the garlic for 3 to 4 min.
2. Stir in the broth and let them cook for 16 min over low heat.
3. Stir in the tomatoes, onion, bell pepper and herbs. Let them cook for 12 min.
4. Spoon the sauce over the spaghetti then serve it hot.
5. Enjoy.

MEXICAN
Spaghetti with Corn Casserole

Prep Time: 10 mins
Total Time: 1 hr 10 mins

Servings per Recipe: 4
Calories	697.9
Fat	29.0g
Cholesterol	67.8mg
Sodium	1121.9mg
Carbohydrates	86.7g
Protein	28.4g

Ingredients

8 oz. spaghetti, broken into 4 parts
2 C. mild cheddar cheese, shredded
1 (15 1/4 oz.) cans cream-style corn
1 (15 1/4 oz.) cans whole kernel corn, drained
2 tbsp margarine, melted
1 C. milk

Directions

1. Before you do anything, preheat the oven to 350 F.
2. Stir corn with milk and 1 1/2 C. of cheese in a baking dish.
3. Stir in the spaghetti and push it down to cover it with the mix. Top it with cheese.
4. Drizzle the melted margarine on top. Lay a loose sheet of oil on top to cover it.
5. Place the dish in the oven and let it cook for 60 min. Serve it hot.
6. Enjoy.

Healthier
Turkey Lasagna

🍲 Prep Time: 15 mins
🕐 Total Time: 1 hr 45 mins

Servings per Recipe: 8
Calories	263 kcal
Carbohydrates	24 g
Cholesterol	74 mg
Fat	9.2 g
Protein	25.4 g
Sodium	663 mg

Ingredients

1 (10 oz) package frozen chopped spinach, thawed and drained
1 C. low-fat cottage cheese
1 egg
cooking spray
1 onion, chopped
2 large garlic cloves, minced
2 C. chopped mushrooms
1 C. shredded carrots
1 lb ground turkey breast
1 (26 oz) jar low-fat pasta sauce (such as Healthy Request®)

1 C. water
1 tsp dried rosemary, minced
1 tsp dried oregano
1 tsp dried basil
6 no-boil lasagna noodles
1 C. shredded low-fat mozzarella cheese
1 C. tomato-vegetable juice cocktail

Directions

1. Set your oven to 400 degrees before doing anything else.
2. Coat a baking dish with nonstick spray.
3. With non-stick spray stir fry: carrots, onions, mushrooms, basil, rosemary, and oregano, and garlic for 5 mins. Combine in your turkey. Fry for another 5 mins. Finally add some water and tomato sauce. Lightly simmer for 10 mins.
4. Create the following layers: 1/3 of sauce, 1/2 lasagna noodles, 1/3 more of sauce, spinach, 1/2 mozzarella. Add rest of lasagna, veggie juice, and garnish with remaining mozzarella.
5. Cook for 45 mins, covered, with foil, then 10 mins without covering.
6. Enjoy.

NO-NOODLE
Lasagna

Prep Time: 20 mins
Total Time: 45 mins

Servings per Recipe: 8
Calories	461 kcal
Carbohydrates	35.3 g
Cholesterol	118 mg
Fat	20.3 g
Protein	32 g
Sodium	975 mg

Ingredients

1 lb ground beef
1 (26 oz) jar spaghetti sauce
1/2 tsp garlic powder
3 C. cooked rice, cooled
2 eggs, lightly beaten

3/4 C. shredded Parmesan cheese, divided
2 1/4 C. shredded mozzarella cheese
2 C. cottage cheese

Directions

1. Set your oven to 375 degrees before doing anything else.
2. Fry your beef until browned for 8 mins, and remove excess grease. Combine in your tomato sauce and also garlic powder.
3. Get a bowl, mix: 1/4 C. parmesan, whisked eggs, and rice.
4. Get a 2nd bowl, mix: 1/4 C. parmesan, cottage cheese, and 2 C. mozzarella
5. Layer the following in a dish: 1/2 rice, 1/2 cheese mix, 1/2 meat. Continue until dish is full. Then top with more mozzarella.
6. Cook for 25 mins, until sauce is simmering, and cheese melted.

No-Bake
3 Cheese Lasagna

Prep Time: 30 mins
Total Time: 2 hrs 30 mins

Servings per Recipe: 10
Calories   521 kcal
Carbohydrates   50.3 g
Cholesterol   110 mg
Fat   20.6 g
Protein   33.1 g
Sodium   861 mg

Ingredients

1 (16 oz) package lasagna noodles
1 lb lean ground beef
1 1/2 (26 oz) jars spaghetti sauce
2 C. shredded mozzarella cheese
1/2 C. grated Parmesan cheese

1 (8 oz) container ricotta cheese
2 eggs
2 C. shredded mozzarella cheese

Directions

1. Boil lasagna in salted water for 7 min until al dente. Remove all water.
2. Fry your beef until brown, remove oil excess, mix in tomato sauce, simmer for 5 mins. Turn off heat.
3. Get a bowl, mix: beaten eggs, 2 C. mozzarella, ricotta, and parmesan.
4. Place half of your beef into the slow cooker first, then some lasagna noodles. Then 1/4 of the cheese mix, then 1/4 more sauce. Continue adding layers until nothing is lest. Topmost layer should be 2 C. of mozzarella.
5. Set slow cooker to high for 3 hours. Then set heat to low for 8 hours.
6. Enjoy.

GARDEN
Lasagna III (Broccoli, Carrots, & Corn)

Prep Time: 30 mins
Total Time: 1 hr 10 mins

Servings per Recipe: 10
Calories	534 kcal
Carbohydrates	48.8 g
Cholesterol	103 mg
Fat	27 g
Protein	26.6 g
Sodium	1091 mg

Ingredients

1 box lasagna noodles
2 eggs, beaten
1 box part-skim ricotta cheese
2 cans condensed cream of mushroom soup
2 C. shredded Cheddar cheese
1 C. grated Parmesan cheese
1 C. sour cream

1 package herb and garlic soup mix
1 bag chopped frozen broccoli, thawed
1 bag frozen sliced carrots
1 bag frozen corn kernels

Directions

1. Set your oven to 375 degrees before anything else.
2. Boil noodles in water with salt for 10 mins. Remove all water, set aside.
3. Get a bowl, mix: soup mix, beaten eggs, sour cream, ricotta, parmesan, cheddar, and mushroom soup.
4. In your baking layer everything in the following manner: lasagna, cheese mix, carrots, corn, broccoli. Continue until all ingredients used. Cheese should be upmost layer.
5. Cook for 30, with a cover of foil. 10 mins without.
6. Enjoy.

Pretty Easy
Lasagna

🥣 Prep Time: 15 mins

🕐 Total Time: 40 mins

Servings per Recipe: 8

Calories	386 kcal
Carbohydrates	29.6 g
Cholesterol	46 mg
Fat	19.3 g
Protein	22.1 g
Sodium	1135 mg

Ingredients

2 C. uncooked penne pasta
1 lb ground Italian chicken sausage
1 (26 oz) jar spaghetti sauce
1 C. cottage cheese

2 C. shredded mozzarella cheese, divided

Directions

1. Set your oven to 350 degrees before doing anything else.

2. Boil your pasta for 8 mins in water and salt. While stir frying your Italian sausage for 10 mins. Then remove oil excesses. Combine pasta, and tomato sauce, with your sausage. And simmer the mix for 3 mins.

3. Now coat a baking dish with nonstick spray. And layer 1/2 of the sauce and pasta at the bottom. Add a layer of cottage cheese, 1/2 mozzarella, add the rest of the pasta. Finally add the rest of the mozzarella.

4. Bake for 30 mins covered with foil. 5 mins without a covering.

5. Enjoy.

MICROWAVE
Mexican Lasagna

Prep Time: 10 mins
Total Time: 25 mins

Servings per Recipe: 10
Calories	709 kcal
Carbohydrates	35.8 g
Cholesterol	143 mg
Fat	45.4 g
Protein	39.3 g
Sodium	1304 mg

Ingredients

11 oz lasagna noodles
1 lb lean ground beef
24 oz tomato sauce
1/2 C. water
1 (1 oz) package taco seasoning mix

8 C. shredded Cheddar cheese
1/2 C. minced tortilla chips

Directions

1. Boil your pasta for 10 mins in water and salt. Remove all water. Set aside.
2. Fry your beef until browned, and remove excess oils. Combine in some taco seasoning, then tomato and finally water. Lightly simmer for 6 mins.
3. Get your dish (must be able to fit in microwave), and layer in the following manner: lasagna noodles, beef mix, cheese. Continue until dish is full.
4. Microwave for 10 mins on the highest power setting covered with plastic wrap.
5. Garnish with tortilla chips.
6. Enjoy.

Italian
Seashells Salad

🥣 Prep Time: 10 mins
🕐 Total Time: 2 hrs 5 mins

Servings per Recipe: 6
Calories   218 kcal
Fat   11.4 g
Carbohydrates   20.4g
Protein   9.6 g
Cholesterol   18 mg
Sodium   654 mg

Ingredients

1 C. seashell pasta
1 C. chopped, cooked chicken meat
3 green onions, chopped into 1 inch pieces
1 red bell pepper, chopped
1 C. sliced black olives
1 cucumber, peeled and chopped

2/3 C. Italian-style salad dressing
1/4 C. sunflower seeds (optional)

Directions

1. Cook the pasta according to the directions on the package.
2. Get a large mixing bowl: Stir in it the pasta, chicken, green onions, bell pepper, olives and cucumber.
3. Drizzle the Italian dressing on top. Toss the salad to coat. Place the salad in the fridge for 3 h. Garnish it with some sunflower seeds then serve it.
4. Enjoy.

Italian Seashells Salad   45

HERMOSA RANCH
Pasta Salad

Prep Time: 35 mins
Total Time: 35 mins

Servings per Recipe: 6
Calories	842.4
Fat	52.7g
Cholesterol	261.0mg
Sodium	1397.4mg
Carbohydrates	65.3g
Protein	30.0g

Ingredients

2 C. uncooked seashell pasta noodles
3 eggs, hard boiled and peeled
1 (3 oz.) packages pepperoni, sliced
1 (8 oz.) packages cheddar cheese, shredded
1 medium size zucchini, chopped
2 - 3 bunches green onions, sliced
Dressing
2 tbsp dry hidden valley ranch dressing mix
1/3 C. milk

1 C. mayonnaise
2 tsp mustard
1/2 tsp sugar
1/4 tsp celery seed
1/4 tsp salt
1/8 tsp pepper
1/8 tsp oregano

Directions

1. Prepare the noodles by following the instructions on the package. Drain it.
2. Get a mixing bowl: Whisk in it the ranch dressing with milk, mayo, sugar, celery seed, oregano, salt and pepper.
3. Get a mixing bowl: Toss in it the noodles with chopped eggs and dressing.
4. Place the salad in the fridge for at 1cast 1 h then serve it.
5. Enjoy.

Mexican Style
Rotini Salad

Prep Time: 15 mins
Total Time: 25 mins

Servings per Recipe: 12
Calories	246 kcal
Fat	5.5 g
Carbohydrates	41g
Protein	8.8 g
Cholesterol	5 mg
Sodium	651 mg

Ingredients

1 (16 oz) package tri-color rotini pasta
1 (15 oz) can black beans, drained and rinsed
1 (11 oz) can Mexican-style corn, drained
1 (4 oz) can chopped green chilies
1/2 C. chopped red bell pepper
1/2 C. Italian-style salad dressing, or more to taste
1/2 C. shredded Mexican cheese blend

3 green onions, thinly sliced
1/3 C. minced fresh cilantro
1 slice onion, minced
2 tbsp taco seasoning mix
1/2 lime, juiced

Directions

1. Cook the pasta according to the directions on the package.
2. Get a large mixing bowl: Combine in it the black beans, corn, green chilies, red bell pepper, Italian dressing, Mexican cheese, green onions, cilantro, onion, taco seasoning, and lime juice together.
3. Stir them well. Fold in the pasta. Adjust the seasoning of the salad then serve it.
4. Enjoy.

FRENCH
Taco Spirals Salad

Prep Time: 10 mins
Total Time: 40 mins

Servings per Recipe: 6
Calories	618 kcal
Fat	38.4 g
Carbohydrates	46.4g
Protein	22.8 g
Cholesterol	68 mg
Sodium	980 mg

Ingredients

2 C. spiral pasta
1 lb ground beef
1 (1.25 oz) package taco seasoning
3 C. shredded lettuce
2 C. halved cherry tomatoes
1 C. shredded Cheddar cheese

1/2 C. chopped onion
1/2 C. French salad dressing
1 (7 oz) bag corn chips
2 tbsp sour cream

Directions

1. Cook the pasta according to the directions on the package.
2. Place a large pan over medium heat. Brown in it the beef for 12 min. Discard the excess grease. Add the taco seasoning and mix them well.7
3. Get a large mixing bowl: Transfer to it the beef mix with pasta; toss lettuce, tomatoes, Cheddar cheese, onion, French dressing, and corn chips.
4. Stir them well. Serve your salad with some sour cream.
5. Enjoy.

Italian
Spring Pasta Salad

Prep Time: 20 mins
Total Time: 20 mins

Servings per Recipe: 8
Calories   233 kcal
Fat   12.2 g
Carbohydrates   26.2g
Protein   6.6 g
Cholesterol   9 mg
Sodium   598 mg

Ingredients

8 oz rotelle or spiral pasta, cooked and drained
(broccoli, carrots, tomatoes, bell peppers, cauliflower, onions and mushrooms)
1/2 C. cubed Cheddar or mozzarella cheese

2 1/2 C. assorted cut-up vegetables
1/3 C. sliced pitted ripe olives (optional)
1 C. Wish-Bone(R) Italian Dressing

Directions

1. Get a large mixing bowl: Combine in it the pasta with veggies, cheddar cheese and olives. Toss them well.
2. Drizzle the dressing on top. Adjust the seasoning of the salad and serve it.
3. Enjoy.

FRUITY
Salmon Macaroni Salad with Yogurt Dressing

Prep Time: 10 mins
Total Time: 40 mins

Servings per Recipe: 8
Calories	222 kcal
Fat	12.3 g
Carbohydrates	17.6 g
Protein	11 g
Cholesterol	18 mg
Sodium	208 mg

Ingredients

1 C. dry pasta, such as macaroni or small shells
8 oz cooked, skinned salmon
1/2 C. minced red or yellow onion
1 C. diced celery
1 medium red apple, diced
1/2 C. chopped walnuts or dry-roasted, unsalted peanuts
Dressing:
1 (6 oz) container fat-free yogurt

2 tbsp olive oil
1 tbsp curry powder
2 tsp fresh lemon juice
2 cloves garlic, crushed
1 tsp Dijon mustard
1/2 tsp salt (or to taste)
Freshly ground black pepper, to taste

Directions

1. Cook the pasta according to the directions on the package.
2. Get a small mixing bowl: Combine in it the dressing ingredients. Mix them well.
3. Get a large mixing bowl: Combine in it the salad ingredients. Add the dressing and stir them well.
4. Adjust the seasoning of the salad. Place it in the fridge until ready to serve.
5. Enjoy.

Balsamic
Romaine Shells Salad

🥣 Prep Time: 20 mins
🕐 Total Time: 30 mins

Servings per Recipe: 9
Calories   312 kcal
Fat   14.7 g
Carbohydrates   30.7g
Protein   14.3 g
Cholesterol   32 mg
Sodium   819 mg

Ingredients

18 jumbo pasta shells
1/2 lb thinly sliced beef salami
4 C. chopped romaine lettuce
1 C. chopped roma tomatoes
3/4 C. seeded and chopped cucumber
3/4 C. chopped red onion

1/2 C. balsamic vinaigrette salad dressing
1 C. shredded Parmesan cheese

Directions

1. Cook the pasta according to the directions on the package.
2. Get a large mixing bowl: Toss in it the pasta with salami, romaine lettuce, roma tomatoes, cucumber, and red onion. Drizzle the balsamic vinegar on top.
3. Mix them well. Spoon the mix into the pasta shells to stuff them with it. Place the pasta shells on a serving shallow bowl. Sprinkle the cheese on top then serve it.
4. Enjoy.

FRUITY
Curry Shells Salad

Prep Time: 25 mins
Total Time: 1 hr 40 mins

Servings per Recipe: 8

Calories	374 kcal
Fat	32.2 g
Carbohydrates	17.6g
Protein	5.1 g
Cholesterol	10 mg
Sodium	515 mg

Ingredients

8 slices turkey bacon
1/2 C. uncooked shell pasta
2 tbsp white vinegar
1/4 C. white sugar
1 1/2 tbsp dried basil
1 tbsp dried thyme
4 cloves garlic, peeled
1 tsp salt
1 tsp curry powder
1/2 tsp ground black pepper

1 C. canola oil
4 peaches, peeled and cut into chunks
1/2 C. chopped fresh parsley
1/2 C. sliced celery
1/2 C. chopped red bell pepper
6 green onions, chopped

Directions

1. Place a large pan over medium heat. Cook in it the bacon for 12 min until it becomes crisp.
2. Remove it from the grease and place it aside to drain and lose heat. Press the bacon until it becomes crumbled and place it aside.
3. Cook the pasta according to the directions on the package.
4. Get a food processor: Combine in it the vinegar, sugar, basil, thyme, garlic, salt, curry powder, and black pepper. Process them until they become smooth.
5. Add to it the oil in a steady stream while blending all the time until the dressing becomes creamy.
6. Get a large mixing bowl: Toss in it the pasta with bacon, dressing, peaches, parsley, celery, red bell pepper, and green onions.
7. Adjust the seasoning of the salad. Place the salad in the fridge for 1 h 10 min then serve it. Enjoy.

Garbanzo
Bows Pasta

🥣 Prep Time: 18 mins
🕐 Total Time: 30 mins

Servings per Recipe: 10
Calories   207 kcal
Fat   14.5 g
Carbohydrates   15.5g
Protein   4.5 g
Cholesterol   11 mg
Sodium   414 mg

Ingredients

2 1/2 C. bow tie (farfalle) pasta
1 C. Greek salad dressing
2 1/2 tbsp mayonnaise
4 radishes, finely chopped

1/2 cucumber, peeled and chopped
1 (15 oz) can garbanzo beans, drained
3/4 C. crumbled feta cheese

Directions

1. Cook the pasta according to the directions on the package.
2. Get a large mixing bowl: Combine in it the Greek dressing and mayonnaise. Mix them well. Stir in the pasta.
3. Add the radishes, cucumber, garbanzo beans, and crumbled feta cheese and stir them gently. Adjust the seasoning of the salad then serve it.
4. Enjoy.

BROCCOLI
Romano Ravioli Salad

Prep Time: 15 mins
Total Time: 30 mins

Servings per Recipe: 4
Calories	653 kcal
Fat	31.7 g
Carbohydrates	66.9g
Protein	28 g
Cholesterol	63 mg
Sodium	902 mg

Ingredients

2 (9 oz) packages BUITONI(R) Refrigerated Light Four Cheese Ravioli, prepared according to package directions, chilled
1/4 C. extra virgin olive oil
4 large cloves garlic, finely chopped
1/4 C. apple cider vinegar
2 medium tomatoes, chopped
2 C. broccoli florets
1 large green bell pepper, chopped

1/2 C. pitted and halved ripe olives
1/2 C. BUITONI(R) Refrigerated Freshly Shredded Parmesan Cheese
1/4 C. BUITONI(R) Refrigerated Freshly Shredded Romano Cheese

Directions

1. Place a large saucepan over medium heat: Heat the oil in it. Add the garlic and cook it for 60 min.
2. Get a large mixing bowl: Transfer the garlic mix to it and allow it to lose heat for few minutes. Add the vinegar and mix them well.
3. Combine in the pasta, tomatoes, broccoli, bell pepper, olives, Parmesan cheese and Romano cheese. Mix them well.
4. Adjust the seasoning of the pasta. Serve it right away.
5. Enjoy.

Cocktail
Shrimp Macaroni Salad

y

Prep Time: 20 mins
Total Time: 1 hr 30 mins

Servings per Recipe: 6
Calories	528 kcal
Fat	41 g
Carbohydrates	31.9g
Protein	9.5 g
Cholesterol	56 mg
Sodium	920 mg

Ingredients

1/2 (12 oz) package elbow macaroni
2 stalks celery, coarsely chopped
1 onion, finely chopped
1 cucumber - peeled, seeded, and diced
1 tomato, diced
1 C. cooked small shrimp

1 C. Italian salad dressing
1 C. mayonnaise, or to taste

Directions

1. Cook the pasta according to the directions on the package.
2. Get a large mixing bowl: Combine in it the pasta with celery, onion, cucumber, tomato, shrimp, and Italian salad dressing.
3. Place the salad in the fridge for 1 h 30 min. Stir in the mayo. Adjust the seasoning of the salad then serve it right away.
4. Enjoy.

Cocktail Shrimp Macaroni Salad 55

TRI-COLORED
Greek Style Pasta Salad

Prep Time: 30 mins
Total Time: 5 hrs 10 mins

Servings per Recipe: 8
Calories	248 kcal
Fat	12.7 g
Carbohydrates	24.9 g
Protein	9 g
Cholesterol	9 mg
Sodium	482 mg

Ingredients

1/2 red onion, cut into bite-size pieces
4 C. ice water, or as needed
1 (8 oz) package tri-color rotini pasta
1 (5 oz) can light tuna in water, drained and flaked
2 stalks celery, cut into bite-size pieces
1/2 C. roasted red peppers, drained and chopped
1/4 C. smoked sun-dried tomatoes
1/4 C. crumbled feta cheese

1 sprig parsley, stemmed and leaves minced
4 leaves fresh basil, rolled and very thinly sliced
2 tsp capers
1 C. Greek vinaigrette salad dressing

Directions

1. Get a large bowl and fill it with ice water. Place the red onion in it and place it in the fridge for 35 min. Remove the onion from the water.

2. Cook the pasta according to the directions on the package.

3. Get a large mixing bowl: Combine in it the onion, pasta, tuna, celery, roasted red peppers, sun-dried tomatoes, feta cheese, parsley, basil, capers, and Greek dressing.

4. Stir them well. Place the salad in the fridge for 5 h to an overnight. Serve your salad with your favorite toppings.

5. Enjoy.

Hot
Pasta Spirals Salad

Prep Time: 20 mins
Total Time: 2 hrs 30 mins

Servings per Recipe: 8
Calories	190 kcal
Fat	7.4 g
Carbohydrates	27.1g
Protein	4.7 g
Cholesterol	0 mg
Sodium	336 mg

Ingredients

1 (8 oz) package pasta spirals
1/4 C. diced sweet onion
1 green bell pepper, seeded and minced
1/2 fresh hot chile pepper, seeded and minced
2 tomatoes, seeded and chopped
1 cucumber, seeded and chopped
1/4 C. olive oil
1/4 C. tomato sauce
1/4 C. lime juice

3 tbsp apple cider vinegar
1 tsp garlic powder
1 tsp salt
ground black pepper to taste

Directions

1. Cook the pasta according to the directions on the package.
2. Get a small mixing bowl: Combine in it the olive oil, tomato sauce, lime juice, apple cider vinegar, garlic powder, salt, and black pepper. Mix them well to make the dressing.
3. Get a large mixing bowl: Combine in tit the pasta, sweet onion, green bell pepper, chile pepper, tomatoes, and cucumber.
4. Drizzle the dressing on top and toss the salad well. Adjust the seasoning of the salad and place it in the fridge for 2 h 30 min then serve it.
5. Enjoy.

ROTINI
Crabmeat Salad

Prep Time: 10 mins
Total Time: 30 mins

Servings per Recipe: 12
Calories	178 kcal
Fat	2 g
Carbohydrates	33.6g
Protein	6.2 g
Cholesterol	4 mg
Sodium	373 mg

Ingredients

1 (12 oz) package rotini pasta
1 (10 oz) package frozen peas, thawed
1 (8 oz) can water chestnuts, chopped
1 (8 oz) package imitation crabmeat,
coarsely chopped - or more to taste

1 C. reduced-fat mayonnaise
2 tbsp chopped fresh chives
1 tbsp chopped fresh dill

Directions

1. Cook the pasta according to the directions on the package.
2. Get a large mixing bowl: Combine in it all the ingredients. Toss them well. Adjust the seasoning of the salad then serve it.
3. Enjoy.

Greek
Rotini Salad with Lemon Dressing

🥣 Prep Time: 20 mins
🕐 Total Time: 9 hrs 33 mins

Servings per Recipe: 8

Calories	453 kcal
Fat	24.9 g
Carbohydrates	50g
Protein	8.9 g
Cholesterol	8 mg
Sodium	1539 mg

Ingredients

1 (16 oz) package tri-color rotini pasta
3 1/2 tbsp lemon juice
2 1/2 tbsp canola oil
3/4 C. mayonnaise
2 1/2 tbsp seasoned salt
1 1/4 tsp flavor enhancer
2 cucumbers, seeded and diced
2 tomatoes, seeded and diced
1 (5 oz) jar sliced pimento-stuffed green olives

1 (3 oz) can chopped black olives
1/4 C. chopped green bell pepper
1/4 C. chopped green onions

Directions

1. Cook the pasta according to the directions on the package.
2. Get a small mixing bowl: Combine in it the lemon juice and canola oil. Mix them well. Add the mayonnaise, seasoned salt, and flavor enhancer then mix them again.
3. Get a large mixing bowl: Toss in it the pasta with dressing. Place it the fridge for an overnight.
4. Add the cucumbers, tomatoes, green olives, black olives, green bell pepper, and green onions to the pasta mix. Toss them well.
5. Adjust the seasoning of the salad then serve it.
6. Enjoy.

FRENCH INSPIRED
Noodles

Prep Time: 30 mins
Total Time: 2 hrs 30 mins

Servings per Recipe: 9
Calories	613.0
Fat	31.2g .
Cholesterol	143.3mg
Sodium	985.3mg
Carbohydrates	36.2g
Protein	38.9g

Ingredients

1/3 C. all-purpose flour
2 tsp salt, divided
3/4 tsp black pepper, divided
2 1/4 lb. beef stew meat
3 turkey bacon, slices chopped and divided
1 C. onion, chopped
1 C. carrot, sliced
4 garlic cloves, minced
1 1/2 C. water

1 (14 oz.) cans beef broth
8 C. mushrooms, halved
2 tbsp tomato paste
2 tsp thyme
2 bay leaves
1 (16 oz.) packages frozen pearl onions
7 C. egg noodles, cooked
3 tbsp parsley

Directions

1. In a zip-top plastic bag, add the beef, flour, 1 tsp of the salt and 1/4 tsp of the black pepper and seal the bag, then shake to coat completely.
2. Heat a large Dutch oven on medium-high heat cook half of the bacon till browned completely. Transfer the bacon onto a paper towel lined plate to drain.
3. In the same skillet, add the beef and cook for about 5 minutes.
4. Transfer the beef onto a plate and cover everything with some foil to keep warm.
5. Repeat with the remaining bacon and beef.
6. In the same pan, add the carrot, onion and garlic and sauté for about 5 minutes.
7. Stir in the broth and water and with the spoon scrape the pan to loosen any browned bits.
8. Add the beef, bacon, salt, black pepper and remaining ingredients except the noodles and parsley and bring to a boil. Reduce the heat and simmer, covered for about 45 minutes.
9. Uncover and simmer for about 1 hour.
10. Remove everything from the heat and discard the bay leaves.
11. Place the beef mixture over the noodles and serve with a topping of the parsley.

Wednesday's
Dinner

🥣 Prep Time: 15 mins
🕐 Total Time: 45 mins

Servings per Recipe: 4
Calories	904.4
Fat	23.9g
Cholesterol	233.9mg
Sodium	1740.2mg
Carbohydrates	96.2g
Protein	74.5g

Ingredients

2 lb. any type boneless skinless chicken
1 (12 oz.) packages egg noodles
2 (10 3/4 oz.) cans cream of chicken soup
1/2 C. milk
1 (10 oz.) packages frozen green peas
1 - 2 tbsp olive oil

8 oz. canned mushrooms
1 small onion, finely chopped
1 tsp minced garlic
1 tsp fresh ground black pepper

Directions

1. In a pan, heat about 1 tbsp of the oil and cook the chicken till done completely.
2. Transfer the chicken into a bowl, then cut it into bite sized pieces.
3. In the same pan, heat the remaining oil on medium-high heat, sauté the onion, mushrooms and garlic till tender.
4. Drain the excess grease from the pan.
5. Stir in the chicken, milk, chicken soup, peas and black pepper and simmer everything for about 15 minutes.
6. Meanwhile, prepare the egg noodles according to the package's directions. Drain well.
7. Add the noodles to the pan with the chicken mixture and gently, stir to combine. Serve the dinner with some biscuits or rolls.

EGGY-WEGGY
Noodle Bake

Prep Time: 15 mins
Total Time: 1 hr 25 mins

Servings per Recipe: 9

Calories	336 kcal
Fat	16.5 g
Carbohydrates	26.2g
Protein	20.9 g
Cholesterol	84 mg
Sodium	744 mg

Ingredients

1 tbsp olive oil
1 lb. extra lean ground beef
1/2 tsp ground dried thyme
1 (1.5 oz.) envelope spaghetti sauce
seasoning mix
1 (6 oz.) can tomato paste
3 C. water
salt and black pepper to taste

1 (8 oz.) package egg noodles
1 (3 oz.) package cream cheese, softened
1 tbsp chopped fresh parsley
1/4 C. grated Parmesan cheese
1 (8 oz.) container sour cream
1 C. shredded mozzarella cheese, divided

Directions

1. In a large skillet, heat the oil on medium-high heat and stir fry the beef for about 5-7 minutes. Drain the excess grease from the skillet.
2. Stir in the tomato paste, spaghetti sauce seasoning mix, thyme, salt, black pepper and water and bring to a boil.
3. Reduce heat to medium-low and simmer, covered for about 25 minutes, stirring occasionally.
4. Set your oven to 350 degrees F and grease a 13x9-inch baking dish.
5. Meanwhile in a large pan of lightly salted boiling water, cook the egg noodles for about 5 minutes.
6. Drain them well and keep everything aside.
7. In a bowl, add the cream cheese, Parmesan and parsley and mix till smooth.
8. Stir in the 3/4 of the shredded mozzarella cheese and sour cream.
9. In the bottom of the prepared baking dish, place half of the noodles, followed by the half of the beef mixture and half of the cream cheese mixture.
10. Repeat the layers once and top with the remaining mozzarella cheese.
11. Cook everything in the oven for about 35 minutes.

Chicken
and Onion Egg Noodle Dump Dinner

🥣 Prep Time: 30 mins
🕐 Total Time: 8 hrs 30 mins

Servings per Recipe: 6
Calories	311 kcal
Fat	3.5 g
Carbohydrates	42g
Protein	26.4 g
Cholesterol	93 mg
Sodium	81 mg

Ingredients

4 skinless, boneless chicken breast halves
6 C. water
1 onion, chopped
2 stalks celery, chopped

salt and pepper to taste
1 (12 oz.) package egg noodles

Directions

1. In a slow cooker, add all the ingredients except the noodles.
2. Set the slow cooker on Low and cook, covered for about 6-8 hours.
3. Remove the chicken from the slow cooker and chop into bite-sized pieces.
4. Now, set the slow cooker on High.
5. Stir in the noodles and cook till the noodles are cooked through.
6. Stir in the chicken and serve

NOODLES
Soup Tunisian Style

Prep Time: 15 mins
Total Time: 50 mins

Servings per Recipe: 4
Calories	578.8
Fat	19.1g
Cholesterol	38.3mg
Sodium	1402.6mg
Carbohydrates	77.8g
Protein	578.8

Ingredients

1 tsp cumin seed
1 lb. swiss chard, stems and center ribs chopped and leaves coarsely chopped (reserve separately)
1 medium red onion, chopped
2 large garlic cloves, minced
3 tbsp extra-virgin olive oil
2 tbsp tomato paste

2 quarts rich and flavorful chicken broth
1 - 2 tbsp harissa
1 tbsp fresh lemon juice
1 (19 oz.) can chickpeas, drained & rinsed
4 oz. fine egg noodles
4 lemon wedges, for accompaniment

Directions

1. In a nonstick skillet, toast the cumin seeds on medium heat, stirring continuously.
2. Remove everything from the heat and let it cool completely.
3. In a grinder, grind the cumin seeds till powdered.
4. In a large heavy pot, heat the oil on medium heat and stir fry the chard stems, onion, garlic 1/2 tsp of cumin, salt and black pepper for about 10 minutes. Stir in the tomato paste and stir fry for about 2 minutes.
5. Stir in the broth, lemon juice and harissa and simmer, covered for about 15 minutes.
6. Stir in the chard leaves, noodles, chickpeas and a little salt and simmer, covered for about 5 minutes.
7. Serve hot with a sprinkling of the remaining cumin.

Mock
Hamburger Helper

Prep Time: 5 mins
Total Time: 20 mins

Servings per Recipe: 4
Calories	298.3
Fat	17.3g
Cholesterol	77.1mg
Sodium	303.5mg
Carbohydrates	10.8g
Protein	24.1g

Ingredients

1 lb ground beef
2 onions, chopped
2 (4 oz.) cans mushrooms
1/4 tsp garlic powder
pepper
salt

1 C. beef broth
2 tbsp cornstarch
parmesan cheese
egg noodles

Directions

1. In a large pan of lightly salted boiling water, cook the egg noodles for about 10-12 minutes.
2. Drain them well and keep everything aside.
3. Heat a large skillet and cook the beef with mushrooms and onions till browned completely.
4. Stir in the broth, garlic, salt and black pepper and simmer for about 10 minutes.
5. Stir in the cornstarch.
6. Place the beef mixture over the noodles and serve with a topping of cheese.

POLISH
Noodles

Prep Time: 5 mins
Total Time: 25 mins

Servings per Recipe: 4

Calories	563.9
Fat	16.6g
Cholesterol	126.2mg
Sodium	138.5mg
Carbohydrates	86.9g
Protein	17.3g

Ingredients

4 C. cabbage (sliced)
1 small onion (chopped)
1/4 C. butter
1 lb wide egg noodles

salt and pepper
sour cream

Directions

1. In large pan of boiling water, prepare the egg noodles according to the package's directions.
2. Drain well.
3. Meanwhile in a large skillet, melt the butter and sauté the onion till tender.
4. Stir in the cabbage and sauté for about 5 minutes.
5. Add the noodles, sour cream, salt and black pepper and mix well.

Chinese
Noodle Salad

🥣 Prep Time: 10 mins
🕐 Total Time: 20 mins

Servings per Recipe: 4
Calories   322.9
Fat   10.9g
Cholesterol   43.2mg
Sodium   505.0mg
Carbohydrates   46.7g
Protein   11.5g

Ingredients

4 C. egg noodles, cooked
1 large avocado, cubed
1 C. imitation crabmeat, diced
1/2 C. water chestnut, chopped (canned)
1 red bell pepper, diced
1 tbsp horseradish cream

1/2 C. low-fat mayonnaise
1 tbsp fresh parsley, finely chopped
1 tbsp fresh chives, finely chopped
salt and pepper, to taste

Directions

1. In a large bowl, mix together the noodles, crabmeat, avocado, bell pepper and water chestnuts.
2. In another bowl, add the remaining ingredients and beat till well combined.
3. Pour the dressing over the salad and toss to coat well.

COUNTRY
Egg Noodle Casserole

Prep Time: 20 mins
Total Time: 50 mins

Servings per Recipe: 4
Calories	740.5
Fat	49.5g
Cholesterol	195.3mg
Sodium	772.2mg
Carbohydrates	24.8g
Protein	47.5g

Ingredients

1 lb ground beef
1/2 C. green pepper
1/2 C. onion
1 tsp seasoning salt
1/8 tsp pepper
8 oz. tomato sauce with basic and garlic
4 -6 oz. egg noodles
1 C. cottage cheese

1 C. sour cream
1 1/2 C. shredded sharp cheddar cheese, divided
1/2 C. grated parmesan cheese

Directions

1. Set your oven to 350 degrees F before doing anything else and grease a casserole dish.

2. Heat a large skillet and cook the beef with the green pepper and onion till browned completely.

3. Stir in the tomato sauce and seasoning and simmer for about 5 minutes. Meanwhile prepare the egg noodles according to the package's directions. Drain well.

4. In a bowl, mix together the noodles, sour cream, cottage cheese and 1/2 C. of the cheddar cheese.

5. In the bottom of the prepared casserole dish, place half of the noodles mixture, followed by the beef mixture and the remaining noodle mixture. Top everything with the remaining cheddar cheese and cook everything in the oven for about 20 minutes.

6. Sprinkle the dish with the Parmesan and cook everything in the oven for about 10 minutes.

Butter
Parmesan Noodles

Prep Time: 10 mins
Total Time: 10 mins

Servings per Recipe: 1
Calories	320.6
Fat	14.0g
Cholesterol	78.4mg
Sodium	113.3mg
Carbohydrates	40.6g
Protein	8.1g

Ingredients

1 1/2 C. egg noodles
salt
1 tbsp butter, chopped
flat leaf parsley
fresh ground black pepper

1/4 C. freshly grated parmigiano-reggiano cheese

Directions

1. In a large pan of lightly salted boiling water, cook the egg noodles for about 5 minutes.
2. Drain well and transfer into a bowl.
3. Add the butter and cheese and toss to coat well.
4. Serve with a sprinkling of the parsley and black pepper.

CREAMY
Noodles Milanese

Prep Time: 5 mins
Total Time: 20 mins

Servings per Recipe: 4
Calories   386.8
Fat   19.3g
Cholesterol   95.0mg
Sodium   201.6mg
Carbohydrates   42.1g
Protein   11.4g

Ingredients

8 oz. wide egg noodles
1/4 C. butter or 1/4 C. margarine,
softened
1/2 C. half-and-half (I use non-fat)

1/4 C. grated parmesan cheese
2 1/4 tsp Italian salad dressing mix

Directions

1. In large pan of boiling water, prepare the egg noodles till they reach the desired doneness.
2. Drain well.
3. In a pan of pasta, add the butter and noodles and toss to coat.
4. Add the remaining ingredients and mix till well combined.
5. Serve immediately.

Little Tike
Noodles

Prep Time: 5 mins
Total Time: 20 mins

Servings per Recipe: 6
Calories   157.5
Fat   10.2g
Cholesterol   38.1mg
Sodium   185.0mg
Carbohydrates   11.3g
Protein   5.3g

Ingredients

9 oz. medium egg noodles, uncooked
3 tbsp butter
1/4 tsp seasoning salt
3 tbsp sour cream

1/2 C. freshly grated parmesan cheese

Directions

1. In a large pan of lightly salted boiling water, cook the egg noodles till desired doneness.
2. Drain well and return in the pan.
3. Add the butter and stir to coat well.
4. Stir in the remaining ingredients and serve.

TOMATO SOUP
and Noodles

Prep Time: 10 mins
Total Time: 30 mins

Servings per Recipe: 8
Calories   303.9
Fat   7.2g
Cholesterol   75.3mg
Sodium   251.2mg
Carbohydrates   39.6g
Protein   20.3g

Ingredients

6 C. broad egg noodles, uncooked
1 lb extra lean ground beef
1 C. onion, sliced
1/2 C. green pepper, chopped
1 (10 oz.) cans mushrooms, undrained
1 (10 oz.) cans condensed tomato soup

1/2 C. light cream cheese spread
1 tbsp Worcestershire sauce
fresh parsley, chopped

Directions

1. In large pan of boiling water, prepare the egg noodles according to the package's directions.
2. Drain well.
3. Heat a large skillet on medium heat and cook the beef till browned completely.
4. Drain the excess grease from the skillet.
5. Stir in the peppers and onions and cook till tender.
6. Stir in the remaining ingredients and cook for about 5 minutes.
7. Place the beef mixture over the noodles and serve with a garnishing of the parsley.

Japanese Style
Egg Noodle

🥣 Prep Time: 10 mins
🕐 Total Time: 25 mins

Servings per Recipe: 6
Calories   152.2
Fat   5.4g
Cholesterol   15.9mg
Sodium   896.9mg
Carbohydrates   22.6g
Protein   4.3g

Ingredients

1/4 lb fine dried egg noodles
1 medium red onion, sliced thinly
1 1/2 C. fresh shiitake mushrooms, sliced thinly
1 tbsp vegetable oil
3 tbsp soy sauce
1 tbsp balsamic vinegar

2 tsp brown sugar
1 tsp salt
1 tbsp sesame oil
fresh parsley leaves, to garnish

Directions

1. In a large pan of lightly salted boiling water, cook the egg noodles for about 5 minutes.
2. Drain them well and keep everything aside.
3. In a large skillet, heat the oil and sauté the mushrooms and onion for about 3 minutes.
4. Stir in the noodles, brown sugar, vinegar, soy sauce and salt and toss to coat well.
5. Stir in the sesame oil and serve with a garnishing of parsley.

GNOCCHI
Comfort Food

🍲 Prep Time: 40 mins
🕐 Total Time: 50 mins

Servings per Recipe: 4
Calories	831 kcal
Fat	60.4 g
Carbohydrates	42.9 g
Protein	28.2 g
Cholesterol	306 mg
Sodium	707 mg

Ingredients

2 eggs
1/2 tsp salt
1/8 tbsp ground black pepper
1/8 tsp ground allspice
1 16 oz. container ricotta cheese
1 10 oz. box frozen chopped spinach, thawed and squeezed dry
1 1/4 C. all-purpose flour
2 C. heavy cream

1 pinch ground allspice to taste
2 oz. crumbled Gorgonzola cheese
salt and pepper to taste

Directions

1. In a large bowl, add the eggs, 1/2 tsp of the salt, 1/8 tsp of the pepper and 1/8 tsp of the allspice and beat well.
2. Add the ricotta cheese and spinach and mix till well combined.
3. Add the flour, 1/4 C. at a time and mix till a soft dough forms.
4. Refrigerate, covered till use.
5. Place the dough onto a floured surface and divide into 4 pieces.
6. Roll each piece into 1/2-inch thick ropes and then cut each rope into 1/2-inch pieces.
7. In a large pan of the lightly salted water, cook the gnocchi over high heat for about 3-4 minutes.
8. In a colander, drain the gnocchi and keep aside.
9. Meanwhile in a pan, add the cream and 1 pinch of allspice and bring to a simmer.
10. Remove from the heat and add the Gorgonzola cheese, salt and pepper and beat well.
11. Add the gnocchi and toss to coat well.
12. Serve immediately.

Fiesta
Gnocchi

Prep Time: 30 mins
Total Time: 1 hr 20 mins

Servings per Recipe: 8
Calories   226 kcal
Fat   8.3 g
Carbohydrates   30.1g
Protein   7.1 g
Cholesterol   43 mg
Sodium   1298 mg

Ingredients

1 acorn squash, halved and seeded
2 cloves garlic, pressed
1/2 tsp salt
1 egg
1 C. whole wheat flour
1 C. white flour
7 C. water
1 tbsp salt
1 cube chicken bouillon
1 C. vegetable broth
1/3 tsp rubbed sage

1/4 tsp ground black pepper
1/4 C. cold unsalted butter, cut into small cubes
1/2 C. grated Parmesan cheese

Directions

1. With a knife, make several slits in the acorn squash.
2. Microwave the squash for about 10 minutes.
3. With a fork, scrape the flesh into a bowl.
4. Add the garlic, 1/2 tsp of the salt, egg, and whole wheat flour and mix well.
5. Slowly, add the white flour, in small amounts and mix till a sticky dough forms.
6. Place the dough onto a floured surface and roll into thin ropes, then cut into quarter-sized gnocchi.
7. In a large pan of the lightly salted water, cook the gnocchi till they float to the top.
8. With a slotted spoon, transfer the gnocchi into a large bowl and keep aside.
9. Discard the cooking water, reserving about 1 1/2 C. in the pan and return to the heat.
10. Add the bouillon cube, broth, sage and pepper and bring to a boil.
11. Boil for about 15 minutes.
12. Reduce the heat to medium. And add the butter cubes, one at a time, beating continuously

till melted completely.

13. Return the gnocchi into the mixture and immediately, remove from the heat.

14. Immediately, stir in the Parmesan cheese.

15. Keep the pan, covered for about 10 minutes before serving.

Restaurant Style
Gnocchi

🍚 Prep Time: 15 mins
🕐 Total Time: 30 mins

Servings per Recipe: 4
Calories	333 kcal
Fat	14.7 g
Carbohydrates	26.7g
Protein	23.7 g
Cholesterol	198 mg
Sodium	471 mg

Ingredients

1 tbsp butter
1 large onion, thinly sliced
6 mushrooms, sliced
1 tsp brown sugar
1 16 oz. package potato gnocchi
20 peeled and deveined large shrimp
3 tbsp reduced-fat sour cream

1 tsp paprika
1 pinch saffron
salt to taste
2 tbsp shredded fresh basil
1/4 C. grated Parmesan cheese

Directions

1. In a large skillet, melt the butter on medium heat and cook the onion, mushrooms and brown sugar for about 10 minutes, stirring occasionally.
2. Transfer the onion mixture into a bowl and keep aside.
3. In a large pan of the lightly salted water, cook the gnocchi over high heat for about 3 minutes.
4. Drain well and keep warm.
5. Place the same skillet on medium-high heat and cook the shrimp for about 5 minutes.
6. Add the onion mixture, sour cream, paprika and saffron and bring to a gentle simmer.
7. Gently fold in the cooked gnocchi and salt.
8. Transfer the gnocchi into a serving dish and serve with a sprinkling of the shredded basil and Parmesan cheese.

LORY BETH'S
Favorite

Prep Time: 5 mins
Total Time: 25 mins

Servings per Recipe: 4
Calories	706 kcal
Fat	60.4 g
Carbohydrates	23.7g
Protein	17.1 g
Cholesterol	204 mg
Sodium	724 mg

Ingredients

1 lb. gnocchi
1 tbsp olive oil
2 C. chopped radicchio
1 1/2 C. heavy whipping cream

8 oz. Gorgonzola cheese
1/8 tsp ground allspice
salt and ground black pepper to taste

Directions

1. In a large pan of the lightly salted water, cook the gnocchi over high heat for about 2-4 minutes.
2. Drain well.
3. In a skillet, heat the olive oil on medium heat and cook the radicchio for about 5 minutes.
4. Transfer the radicchio into a bowl and with a plastic wrap, cover the bowl, and then keep aside.
5. In the same skillet, add the heavy cream on medium heat and bring to a boil.
6. Simmer for about 5 minutes.
7. Add the Gorgonzola chunks and cook for about 2 minutes, beating continuously.
8. Stir in the radicchio, allspice, salt and black pepper.
9. Add the gnocchi and toss to coat well.

Southern Italian
Country Gnocchi

🥣 Prep Time: 15 mins
🕐 Total Time: 45 mins

Servings per Recipe: 4
Calories	270 kcal
Fat	11 g
Carbohydrates	25.7g
Protein	18.3 g
Cholesterol	130 mg
Sodium	1119 mg

Ingredients

1 lb. fresh basil, stems removed
1 C. ricotta cheese
3/4 C. all-purpose flour, divided
1/2 C. freshly grated Parmigiano-Reggiano
2 egg yolks, lightly beaten
1/4 tsp ground allspice

2 tsp freshly ground white pepper
2 tsp sea salt
1/2 lemon, juiced optional

Directions

1. In a large pan of salted boiling water, cook the basil for about 1 minute.
2. With a slotted spoon transfer the basil in a bowl of the ice water for several minutes to stop the cooking process.
3. Drain well squeeze to dry, then chop finely.
4. In a large bowl, add the ricotta cheese, 1/2 C. of the flour, Parmigiano-Reggiano cheese, egg yolks, allspice, basil, white pepper and salt and mix till well combined.
5. Dust your hands with remaining 1/4 C. flour and make small balls from the mixture.
6. In a large pan of the salted boiling water, add the lemon juice and gnocchi in batches and cook for about 3-4 minutes.
7. Drain well.
8. Serve warm with your favorite sauce.

RUSTIC
Cottage Gnocchi

Prep Time: 20 mins
Total Time: 1 hr 22 mins

Servings per Recipe: 4
Calories	353 kcal
Fat	12.8 g
Carbohydrates	37.9g
Protein	24.6 g
Cholesterol	103 mg
Sodium	1209 mg

Ingredients

1 16 oz. container LACTAIDR Cottage
Cheese
2 eggs
1/2 C. non-dairy Parmesan cheese
substitute
1 tsp salt

1 tsp ground black pepper
1 tsp garlic powder
1 C. all-purpose flour, plus more for
rolling out dough

Directions

1. Arrange a mesh strainer over a bowl.
2. Place the cottage cheese in the mesh strainer and keep aside for about 2 hours, stirring occasionally.
3. Discard the liquid. In a large bowl, add the drained cottage cheese, eggs, non-dairy Parmesan cheese substitute, salt, pepper, garlic powder and flour and mix till a very soft and sticky dough forms.
4. Make a ball with the mixture and lightly dust with the flour.
5. With a plastic wrap, cover the dough ball and refrigerate for about 1 hour. Divide the dough into 4 pieces.
6. Place each dough piece onto a lightly floured surface and roll each piece into a 1/2-inch thick rope.
7. Cut each rope into 1-inch pieces, and arrange onto a lightly floured baking sheet. Roll the gnocchi down the tines of a fork to create the ridges and return them to the baking sheet.
8. Refrigerate till use. In a large pan of the salted boiling water, add the lemon juice and gnocchi in batches and cook for about 2 minutes.
9. Drain well.
10. Serve with your favorite sauce and garnishing.

Sweet Rice
Gnocchi

Prep Time: 30 mins
Total Time: 1 hr 41 mins

Servings per Recipe: 8

Calories	107 kcal
Fat	0.8 g
Carbohydrates	22.6 g
Protein	2.8 g
Cholesterol	23 mg
Sodium	160 mg

Ingredients

1 1/2 lb. potatoes
1 egg at room temperature, lightly beaten
1/3 C. potato starch
1 tbsp sweet rice flour
1/2 tsp fine salt
2 tbsp rice flour

Directions

1. Set your oven to 400 degrees F before doing anything else.
2. With a fork, prick all the potatoes a few times and arrange onto a baking sheet. Cook in the oven for about 50 minutes.
3. Remove from the oven and keep aside to cool for about 10 minutes.
4. Peel the potatoes and pass through a ricer into a large bowl.
5. With a wooden, spoon, create a well in the mashed potatoes.
6. In the well, add the egg and mix well.
7. In another bowl, mix together the potato starch, sweet rice flour and salt. Sprinkle the flour mixture over the potato mixture and stir till a soft dough forms.
8. With a knife, cut the dough into 4 equal portions.
9. Place each dough portion onto a rice flour dusted surface and roll each into a 1-inch thick rope.
10. Cut each rope into 1-inch gnocchi.
11. Gently roll each gnocchi with the back of a fork to create ridges.
12. Shake off any excess rice flour and keep the gnocchi aside for about 5 minutes.
13. In a large pan of the salted boiling water, cook the gnocchi in batches for about 1-2 minutes.
14. With a slotted spoon, transfer into a bowl.
15. Serve with your favorite sauce and garnishing.

SAINT ANNE'S
Feast Gnocchi

🍜 Prep Time: 30 mins
🕐 Total Time: 35 mins

Servings per Recipe: 8
Calories	333.0
Fat	12.3g
Cholesterol	83.3mg
Sodium	497.2mg
Carbohydrates	40.9g
Protein	13.6g

Ingredients

1 C. mashed baking potato
2 eggs
1 tsp salt
1 C. ricotta cheese

8 tsp butter, clarified
1 C. Romano cheese, grated
3 C. flour

Directions

1. In a bowl, add the potato, eggs and salt and beat till fluffy.
2. Add the ricotta cheese, butter, Romano cheese and flour and knead till smooth.
3. Make 1/2-inch rolls from the dough and then cut into 1-inch pieces.
4. With your thumb, make an impression in each piece, then lightly dust with the flour.
5. In a large pan of the boiling salted water, cook the gnocchi till they rise to the surface.
6. Drain well.
7. Mix with your favorite tomato sauce and serve with a garnishing of the grated cheese.

5-Ingredient
Gnocchi

🥣 Prep Time: 30 mins
🕐 Total Time: 1 hr 15 mins

Servings per Recipe: 6
Calories	292.0
Fat	1.3g
Cholesterol	31.0mg
Sodium	22.6mg
Carbohydrates	60.9g
Protein	8.7g

Ingredients

1 kg old potato, cooked & mashed
2 C. all-purpose flour
1 egg, beaten
1 pinch allspice

salt and pepper, to taste

Directions

1. In a bowl, add the mashed potatoes, flour, egg, allspice, salt and pepper and with your fingertips lightly, knead till a firm but soft dough forms.
2. Divide the dough into 4 equal sized pieces.
3. Place the dough pieces onto a lightly floured surface and roll into long sausage shapes.
4. Cut the rolls into small 1-inch pieces.
5. Press each piece over the back of a fork, pressing lightly with 2 fingers.
6. In a large pan of salted boiling water, cook the gnocchi in batches for about 3-4 minutes.
7. With a slotted spoon, transfer into a large bowl.
8. Mix with your favorite pasta sauce and serve with a garnishing of the Parmesan cheese.

WHIPPED
Cream Gnocchi

Prep Time: 20 mins
Total Time: 45 mins

Servings per Recipe: 4
Calories	300.7
Fat	32.0g
Cholesterol	91.0mg
Sodium	383.2mg
Carbohydrates	0.7g
Protein	3.7g

Ingredients

1 lb gnocchi fresh or frozen
1/4 C. mild gorgonzola, crumbled
1/2 C. butter, melted
3 tbsp grated parmesan cheese

1/4 C. whipping cream, warmed
pepper

Directions

1. In a bowl, add the crumbled gorgonzola, melted butter and a pinch of pepper and with a wooden spoon, stir till creamy.
2. Stir in the Parmesan and warm cream.
3. Keep the sauce on very low heat to keep warm.
4. In a large pan of the salted boiling water, cook the gnocchi till they floats to the surface.
5. With a slotted spoon, transfer the gnocchi into a bowl with the sauce and stir well.
6. Serve immediately.

Tuesday's
Lunch

Prep Time: 5 mins
Total Time: 30 mins

Servings per Recipe: 2
Calories	150.2
Fat	14.4g
Cholesterol	41.6mg
Sodium	523.6mg
Carbohydrates	1.9g
Protein	3.9g

Ingredients

1 lb frozen gnocchi
2 tbsp butter
2 garlic cloves, minced
1/4 tsp salt

1/4 tsp pepper
1/4 C. fresh Romano cheese
3 tbsp fresh parsley

Directions

1. Cook gnocchi according to package's instructions.
2. Drain well.
3. In a sauté pan, melt the butter and cook the gnocchi and minced garlic for about 2 minutes, stirring continuously.
4. Stir in salt and pepper and cook for about 2 minutes.
5. Add the Romano cheese and toss to coat and remove from the heat.
6. Serve with a topping of the parsley.

GNOCCHI
Soup 101

Prep Time: 10 mins
Total Time: 35 mins

Servings per Recipe: 8
Calories	236.8
Fat	15.1g
Cholesterol	60.7mg
Sodium	240.6mg
Carbohydrates	8.2g
Protein	16.4g

Ingredients

3 - 4 chicken breasts, cooked and diced
4 C. chicken stock
2 C. half-and-half
1 stalk celery, diced
1 garlic clove, chopped
1/2 carrot, shredded
1/2 onion, diced
1 C. fresh spinach, chopped

1 tbsp olive oil
1 tsp thyme
salt and pepper
16 oz. potato gnocchi
1 tbsp cornstarch optional

Directions

1. In a large skillet, heat the oil and sauté the onion, celery, garlic and carrot till tender.
2. Add the chicken, chicken stock, half and half, salt and pepper, thyme and bring to a boil.
3. Add the gnocchi and gently boil for about 4 minutes.
4. Reduce the heat and simmer for about 10 minutes.
5. Add the spinach and cook for about 1-2 minutes.
6. Meanwhile, dissolve the cornstarch in 1-2 tbsp water
7. Heat to boiling and add cornstarch dissolved in 1-2 tbsp of the water.
8. Add the cornstarch mixture and stir till desired thickness.

How to
Make Gnocchi

🥣 Prep Time: 30 mins
🕐 Total Time: 36 mins

Servings per Recipe: 5
Calories	285.5
Fat	3.9g
Cholesterol	75.5mg
Sodium	491.5mg
Carbohydrates	53.9g
Protein	7.7g

Ingredients

2 C. boiling water
2 C. instant potato flakes
1 tsp salt
2 tsp olive oil

2 beaten egg yolks
2 C. all-purpose flour
1 pinch allspice optional

Directions

1. In a pan of the boiling water, add the salt, oil, and potato flakes and stir till well combined, then immediately, remove from the heat.
2. With a plastic, wrap, cover the pan and keep in the room temperature to cool.
3. After cooling, add the egg yolks and stir to combine well.
4. Place about 2 C. of the all-purpose flour onto a cutting board.
5. Place the potato mixture over the flour and knead till a smooth and slightly sticky dough forms.
6. Cut small piece of the dough and roll out into finger width ropes.
7. Cut each rope into 1/2-inch pieces.
8. Arrange the gnocchi onto a parchment paper lined baking sheet in a single layer and immediately, freeze.
9. After frozen solid, transfer the gnocchi into freezer baggies and freezer till use.
10. Before serving in a large pan of lightly salted boiling water, add the frozen gnocchi and stir to avoid the sticking.
11. Cook till the gnocchi float to the top and then cook for about 2 minutes. Drain well. Serve with your favorite sauce and meatballs.

GNOCCHI
British Style

Prep Time: 10 mins
Total Time: 50 mins

Servings per Recipe: 6
Calories   132.3
Fat   8.8g
Cholesterol   13.2mg
Sodium   242.1mg
Carbohydrates   12.6g
Protein   3.2g

Ingredients

2 tbsp olive oil
3 cloves garlic, minced
1 32 oz. cans plum tomatoes
1 tsp dried basil
1 6 oz. cans tomato paste
1 tbsp chopped fresh parsley
salt and pepper
1/2 C. light cream

2 lbs frozen gnocchi
grated parmesan cheese

Directions

1. In a frying pan, heat the oil and sauté the garlic slightly.
2. In a blender, add the garlic, can of the tomatoes and tomato paste and pulse till smooth.
3. Return the mixture into the pan with the seasonings and simmer for about 30 minutes.
4. Stir in the cream and simmer for about 10 minutes.
5. Place the sauce over the gnocchi and serve with a sprinkling of the grated Parmesan cheese.

Hot
Potato Gnocchi

🥣 Prep Time: 10 mins
🕐 Total Time: 12 mins

Servings per Recipe: 8
Calories   156.6
Fat   1.4g
Cholesterol   46.5mg
Sodium   324.7mg
Carbohydrates   30.2g
Protein   5.2g

Ingredients

2 C. instant potato flakes
1/4 tsp garlic powder
1 tsp salt
2 C. hot water

2 eggs, slightly beaten
1 1/2-2 C. all-purpose flour
oil as needed

Directions

1. In a bowl, add about 3-4 tbsp of the oil, instant potato flakes, garlic powder, salt and hot water and with a spoon, stir till the mixture becomes thick.
2. Add the beaten eggs and mix till well combined.
3. Add in 1-1/2 C. flour and mix till a manageable dough forms.
4. With your hands gently, knead till the dough becomes smooth.
5. With the floured hands, make a ball with a little over 1 tbsp of the dough.
6. In a pan of the boiling water, cook the gnocchi for about 2-3 minutes.
7. With a slotted spoon, transfer the gnocchi into a greased bowl.
8. Serve with your favorite sauce.